saints Who T̶ ̶ ̶ ̶

"*saints* is uniquely effective for helping us realize that we are all called to holiness and sainthood. The stories are immensely readable and presented in relatively short, relatable and actionable ways. Keep this book handy and read it a little every day."
—**Patrick Lencioni,** cofounder of The Amazing Parish and bestselling author of *The Five Dysfunctions of a Team* and *The Advantage*

"In *saints Who Transformed Their World*, Sherry Weddell shares the inspirational stories of relatively unknown lay saints who proclaimed the gospel in creative and unexpected ways. Her purpose is not to present unrealistic hagiographies but to inspire each and every one of us to aspire for radical holiness. These saints changed the world, and with the grace of God, we can too.
—**Sr. Theresa Aletheia Noble, FSP,** author of the *Remember Your Death: Memento Mori* series

"*saints Who Transformed Their World* is a book that will inspire you to live your best life by offering God all you are and have. Sherry Weddell brings the saints to life and, in doing so, offers fresh perspective on how God can work through anyone who is thoroughly abandoned to his will. What she has done for our understanding of our charisms is now taken to an even higher level of practicality as we see how our own spiritual gifts can transform our culture."
—**Lisa Brenninkmeyer,** founder of Walking with Purpose

"Boy, do we need this now. Sherry Weddell has given us a gleaming gem of inspiration and hope. This little book introduces us to holy men and women you may not know—but you will be so grateful you met them! Pick it up, read it, savor it, and pass it on. In a Church hungry for heroes and new disciples, this book shows how others have done it. Don't be surprised if *Saints Who Transformed Their World* transforms your world."
—**Deacon Greg Kandra,** blogger at *The Deacon's Bench*/Patheos.com and author of *The Busy Person's Guide to Prayer*

"A beautiful inspiring book filled with stories of ordinary laypeople saying yes to their gift and using them to change the world! You will want to embrace your gifts and charisms in a whole new way after reading it!"
—**Becky Eldredge,** author of *Busy Lives and Restless Souls: How Prayer Can Help You Find the Missing Peace in Your Life*

"We are all called to use our God-given gifts and talents. Throughout the pages of *saints Who Transformed Their World*, I could see the movement of the Holy Spirit in the lives of eleven amazing laypeople who used their gifts and talents in ways that made the world a better place. Sherry Weddell's book is a must read for everyone—but especially for those who feel as if the Holy Spirit is moving them in a new direction in their lives."
—**Lorene Hanley Duquin,** author of *The Catholic Grandparents Handbook: Creative Ways to Show Love, Share Faith, and Have Fun*

Acknowledgments

I do not recommend trying to finish a book while teaching multi-day seminars around the US and simultaneously prepping a long series of international events in Britain, Australia, and New Zealand. But such was my lot this time round: gentle reader, learn from my mistakes!

Consequently, I feel no shame in admitting that this book would never have seen the light of day without the endless patience, creativity, and dogged but always friendly harassment of Cindy Cavnar, editor and researcher extraordinaire. Cindy walked me through the long process of writing my first book, *Forming Intentional Disciples*, and schlepped me through this book as well. I owe you one, Cindy! (Well . . . more like five, but who's keeping score?)

I must also acknowledge how much I owe the ever-gracious and patient Beth McNamara who helped keep my nose to the grindstone as well. Together with Cindy, she made the impossible possible. Blessings on both your heads!

August 20, 2019
Feast of St. Bernard of Clairvaux

saints

Who Transformed Their World

SHERRY WEDDELL

Published by the Word Among Us Press
7115 Guilford Drive, Suite 100
Frederick, Maryland 21704

23 22 21 20 19 1 2 3 4 5

ISBN: 978-1-59325-355-4
eISBN: 978-1-59325-303-5

Cover design by Faceout Studios
Interior design by Suzanne Earl

Library of Congress Control Number:
2019913385

Contents

Introduction

I come from a tough background, as so many people do. We spend much of our time trying to make sense of the challenges we faced. One of the most crucial healing factors for me was understanding the wholistic, life-restoring power and hope of Jesus' work of redemption, through which the power of sin, Satan, and death are broken in real human lives. I have always been drawn to what the Church calls "subjective redemption"—the earthly drama of how you and I access and then can become channels of Jesus' redemptive, saving power for others in this life.

The charisms that each of us have been given are, in their own way, channels of Jesus' redemptive healing. That is why I often say that "all the charisms are instruments of healing." This reality is one of the primary reasons that I've been helping Catholics discern and exercise their charisms for twenty-five years.

This is also why I am passionate about personal vocation—because when each one of us faithfully answers God's unique call in our lives, *the fruit that you and I bear will be the answer to someone else's prayer*. Maybe many "someones."

I have spent a long time trying to understand why sacraments filled with the power of the redemption seem to be so powerless to change lives. But as I discovered, the Church's teaching on the absolute necessity of "disposition"—of personal faith, spiritual hunger, repentance, and openness to grace and to union with Jesus Christ, our Redeemer—proved to be the missing key!

That why I'm so moved by the Church's teaching on the life-changing power of Eucharistic Adoration. Because there we are in the presence of the glorified Redeemer who is fully present and pouring out his love, graces, and the Holy Spirit on the person who is worshiping and also on God's Church and the world. Saints and theologians have often talked about the incredible healing power of simply spending time with the risen Jesus Christ and of the many instances of spiritual, emotional, and physical healing that have occurred and still occur there today.

That's why I talk so much about the major importance of individual and corporate intercessory prayer, through which the repressive power of corporate sin and Satan is lifted from believers and nonbelievers alike, and the hope of the redemption is revealed and made accessible to us.

Coming from my background, I desperately needed "redeeming truth"—a force more powerful than death and suffering—a divine power that breaks the power and consequences of individual and corporate sin and heals and restores us to God's full purpose for us. I needed it for myself, and I longed to see it made available to others.

There are so many more sources of healing available to us: the healing power of Christian community, the Church's theology of the laity that talks of us restoring the "value of all creation" (*Lumen Gentium*, 36), and the transforming power of Scripture, to name a few. There is an immense tradition of redemption, restoration, and healing within the Catholic faith: complex, rich, and multifaceted. For years, I told others what I told myself: "Seek out and immerse yourselves in as many aspects of healing made available through Jesus Christ as possible."

What we call "the scandals" are, I believe, the painful destruction of one kind of institutionally tolerated corporate and individual sin that has obscured the healing power of Jesus Christ through his Church for centuries. There is a long double obedience involved with profound healing—the persistent seeking out and responding to God's grace on the part of the wounded and the persistent and deep repentance on the part of those responsible for the actions that have wounded so many. Addressing our widespread failure to make disciples and form and nurture disciples is key to both.

The Power of Stories

The pain we are going through now is a new opportunity for the healing power of the Redeemer to be manifest in and through his Church. Jesus, through his union with each one of us, enables us to become small and very partial channels of his immense redemptive work that is being made manifest constantly through his body in the midst of the world. We can draw inspiration from the saints' stories, especially the stories of *lay* saints—those who served in the single or married state, not as priests or religious.

My discovery of the lay saints began when I was a new Catholic. I was asked if I would be interested in coming up with a way to help a local Catholic apostolate's leaders to discern their "charisms," defined as "an extraordinary power given by the Holy Spirit for the good of the Church." I had just finished graduate school and was in the mood to try something new.

I was only vaguely acquainted with the idea of spiritual gifts from my evangelical Protestant upbringing, so I knew that I would have to do some research. The evangelicals I knew as a teenager gave out a "spiritual gifts" inventory to fill out and a one-day workshop to attend and then turned those people loose in their local congregations. It was assumed that the support for ongoing discernment was already present in their church communities.

My experience with the Catholic Church was limited to a single American city, but even I knew that the kind of support common among evangelicals was rare or nonexistent in Catholic parishes. So I spent that summer creating a process for discerning one's charisms that incorporated community discernment and support. The end result was a ten-week spiritual gifts discernment process that I offered for the first time that fall to twenty handpicked leaders.

I already knew that some Catholics were suspicious of ideas that struck them as "foreign" or even "Protestant." It dawned on me that Catholics really trusted saints. If I told the stories of how well-known Catholic saints had discerned and exercised their charisms, I speculated, people would realize that the Church had recognized the importance of the discernment of charisms by all the baptized throughout her history. As St. Pope John Paul II wrote, "Each one, therefore, must be helped to embrace the gift entrusted to him as a completely unique person, and to hear the words which the Spirit of God personally addresses to him" (*Pastores Dabo Vobis*, 40).

So I began my research. I quickly discovered that "saints stories" were so inspiring for me and for my workshop participants that I didn't want to stop! Now I have several floor-to-ceiling bookcases filled with biographies of various saints and saints-in-the-making. As I often say when training leaders to facilitate discernment, "The Holy Spirit is in the details!" What comes through in the concrete details of a saint's life is a vivid portrait of how the grace of God enters the world through the faith and obedience of real people. And through them, the lives and destinies of many others are transformed, and the course of history is changed! I have been especially interested in collecting and sharing the stories of creative, evangelizing saints and lay saints who are not well-known. This is because the vast majority of Catholics are not priests or religious, and they need a wide variety of strong role models to encourage their discernment and sense of personal mission.

To put it very simply, charisms are gifts of the Holy Spirit that we are given so that we can give them away. They are graces given to us, not for our own sake, but *for the sake of others*. Charisms are supernatural graces that pass through you and me—with our assent and cooperation—to convey God's provision, beauty, truth, healing, and mercy to someone else. As *Lumen Gentium* puts it,

> "The manifestation of the Spirit is given to everyone for profit" (cf I Thess 5:12, 19-21). These charisms, whether they be the more outstanding or the most simple and widely diffused, are to be received with thanksgiving and consolation for they are perfectly suited to and useful for the needs of the Church. (12)

It has been an incredible privilege to walk with thousands of Catholics of all ages and walks of life through their discernment process. I have been told again and again by lay Catholics that it was the first time that they had ever talked about their experience of God with someone else. Although I did not design the Called & Gifted process for evangelizing, I discovered that the whole discernment process awakened many to the possibility of a relationship with God in a whole new way. It is also most people's first experience of being supported by the Catholic community as a person called and gifted by God for service to others.

Discerning your charisms nourishes and strengthens spiritual trust, builds spiritual curiosity and openness, and fosters your sense of being personally called by God. I've seen people grow tremendously in confidence and creativity as they accept their own personal baptismal responsibility in the redemptive mission of Jesus Christ. Called & Gifted is usually their first exposure to the Church's theology of the laity's apostolate and personal vocation. Discerning charisms facilitates the emergence of new leadership and initiatives. It also helps foster a larger culture of discernment and the discernment of personal vocations, including priestly and religious vocations.

All charisms are evangelizing in their own way because they make the beauty, provision, compassion, wisdom, healing, and truth of God present. The fruit of a charism removes obstacles to faith and reveals Jesus to believers and nonbelievers.

I have heard so many remarkable and hopeful stories: a young adult cured of terminal cancer by God through another young adult's emerging gift of healing and stories of how the prayers of intercessors have changed the spiritual climate of entire parishes. I have met gifted evangelizers who have been used to introduce Jesus to Muslims and other nonbelievers and skeptics, as well as a retired colonel who offered his pastor two years of free full-time service as parish administrator as a result of discerning a charism of administration.

I have seen professionals leave high-paying careers because they recognized God's call to pastoral work or youth ministry and, paradoxically, parish and diocesan staff returning to the secular marketplace because they recognized that God had called and gifted them as secular apostles. As one young man put it, "You made being a lay apostle sound so interesting!" The Called & Gifted discernment process has also helped many men and women discern a call to religious life.

And then there was the pharmacist who drove to another state to attend a workshop and discerned the charism of missionary. She uprooted her whole life, moved to Africa for three years, and helped change the course of an entire nation by training its leaders to distribute AIDS medication. As one woman in my parish put it, "She's like Esther! She was raised up by God for such a time as this."

Exactly! Our history is filled with the stories of ordinary men and women who have been raised up by God for the people and needs of their times—people through whom God did extraordinary things as they followed Jesus in the midst of his Church. That's why I love making it possible for Catholics to hear and be challenged by the stories of lay saints: women and men whom God has powerfully used as channels of his beauty, mercy, wisdom, healing, and provision, to be received by many others.

The Church teaches that all the baptized are "apostles"—that is, "sent ones," in their own right—that Jesus himself anointed for a mission through Baptism. People have repeatedly told me that *believing this changes everything*: our relationship with God and the Church, with our family, friends, and coworkers—even the meaning of our entire life.

God raised up Madeleine Debrêl, Satoko Kitahara, Joseph Dutton, Georges Vanier, and Antoni Gaudí—they each said "yes!" in their own time and place. The long ripples of their "yes" are still changing lives today. It changes everything to realize that there is someone right now who is waiting to receive the fruit of what you have been given. You may not know them yet. They may not even have been born yet, but in God's intention—in God's Providence—*you* are the one! Just like the lay saints of the past, you have been called and gifted by God for a purpose and for a mission. And just as it did for the men and women described in this book, it *matters* today that *you* say "yes!"

May you hear God's voice calling you through the stories of these blessed servants of God!

CHAPTER ONE

God's Architect
Antoni Gaudí

Charism: Craftsmanship

Born June 25, 1852, in Reus, Spain
Died June 10, 1926, in Barcelona, Spain

Do you want to know where I found my model? An upright tree; it bears its branches and these, in turn, their twigs, and these, in turn, the leaves. And every individual part has been growing harmoniously, magnificently, ever since God the artist created it.

—Antoni Gaudí[1]

On June 7, 1926, the architect Antoni Gaudí left his workshop at the church of Sagrada Família in Barcelona to walk to the nearby church of St. Philip Neri. He was going there to pray—his daily practice—when he was hit by a streetcar as he crossed the tracks on the Gran Via de les Corts Catalanes. No one in the crowd recognized the renowned architect—he carried no identification papers and was so shabbily dressed, untidy, and gaunt that everyone assumed he was homeless. The police took him to the hospital for charity cases. There he lingered, suffering from broken ribs and internal bleeding.

His friends tracked him down the next day, but by then it was too late. In keeping with his long-standing wish to die poor, he refused the offer to move him to a better setting, saying, "Here is where I belong." Two days later, he died. His last words were "Amen, my God, my God."[2]

The Basílica de la Sagrada Família—the Basilica of the Holy Family—is now a UNESCO World Heritage site and one of the most visited tourist destinations in Spain. Under construction since 1882 and not scheduled to be structurally complete until roughly 2026, it is nevertheless a functioning church that hosts weekly Mass and is open daily for prayer. At the same time, it is a testament to the creative genius of Antoni Gaudí, who worked on the project for forty years. Seven of his projects, in fact, have been named World Heritage sites.

As a child, Gaudí struggled with rheumatic fever and its accompanying joint pain, and he spent considerable time recuperating in the countryside. There, immersed in the natural world, he became familiar with the nonlinear forms found in nature—spiderwebs, snail shells, tree trunks with their branching limbs, stems of flowers, blossoms, and leaves. Nature is "the Great Book, always open, that we should force ourselves to read," he once said.[3]

Gaudí's charism for craftsmanship had deep roots—he came from a long line of craftsmen—and he found the shapes of nature mimicked in his family's workshop. His father, grandfather, and great-grandfather were all metalworkers, and the curved pipes and round shapes of the boilers and fittings of their workplace proved to be a lasting influence. Later in life he often said that the memory of those cauldrons and serpentine pipes influenced his "habit of thinking in three dimensions"—so much so that he typically didn't use sketches or make models for his work.[4]

When he was eleven, he entered a local school run by monks. He wasn't much of a student, although he could draw well and had a strong gift for math and geometry. At sixteen, he moved seventy miles away to Barcelona where he completed his secondary education and enrolled in the Provincial School of Architecture. His mediocre academic performance continued there—he skipped classes, finding that the college curriculum prized discipline over creativity.

In spite of his attitude toward class work, he said that he devoured books in the library. Some professors, recognizing his talent, asked him to work with them on their projects. When the time came for him to receive his degree, however, faculty opinion was divided, and he narrowly survived the vote. When the director of the architectural school presented it to him in 1878, he said to those assembled, "I do not know if we have awarded this degree to a madman or to a genius; only time will tell."[5]

Gaudí quickly made a name for himself, landing commissions for houses and other buildings. His style is often classified as Art Nouveau, but in reality his work defies categories. His brilliance lay in part in his ability to capture in stone the forms he found in nature and to embellish his work—both structural and decorative—with color. He adapted the ancient mosaic-like technique known as *trencadís*, for example, using bits of smashed china and broken tile to enliven curved balconies and rooftops and to create the decorative dragons, salamanders, and other forms that were a signature of his work. His affinity for geometry coupled with his insights into the forms of the natural world—tree trunks, for example, or the bones of the human skeleton—enabled him to devise, among other things, new means for supporting heavy walls.

Construction on the Sagrada Família had only just begun when the original architect resigned, and Gaudí agreed to take over management of the project while continuing with his other commissions. He was only thirty-one but wealthy, a bit of a dandy, fond of the opera, and supremely confident in his abilities. His life took a turn, however, when his two attempts to marry failed. The first woman to whom he proposed turned him down because she was already engaged. The second accepted his proposal but then broke the engagement to enter the convent. By this time, his mother and siblings had died, and his father and orphaned niece had come to live with him.

Although a Catholic, he hadn't been particularly religious, but now he began a slow, steady movement toward deeper conversion. He prayed and read the Bible every day, attended daily Mass, made the decision not to marry, and received regular spiritual guidance from several priests. Gaudí fasted—sometimes to excess—gave up alcohol, and became a vegetarian. Still, he never won his lifelong struggle to control his temper, and he could be plainspoken to a fault. "I have to say things exactly as they are, without beating around the bush," he said, "and of course people are annoyed."[6]

Shortly after the deaths of his father and niece, he moved into his workshop at the Sagrada Família. He devoted the last ten years of his life solely to his work there. The church was only one-quarter finished when Gaudí died, but the lofty tree-like columns of the interior and the windows through which lights pours in as if through the canopy of a forest capture the spirit of his work. "Sunshine is the best painter," he once said.[7] Although it is possible to appreciate Gaudí's art apart from his faith, he saw them as inseparable. His work, he said, was a collaboration with the Creator.[8]

In 2000, the Vatican swiftly approved a petition to open Gaudí's cause for canonization—his life as an artist, man of faith, and layman caught the attention of Pope St. John Paul II. In 2010, Pope Benedict XVI came to Barcelona and formally consecrated the church as a basilica. Paying tribute to Gaudí in his homily, Pope Benedict said that he had closed the gap between the beauty of earthly things and "God as beauty."

Gaudí did this, the Pope said, "not with words but with stones, lines, planes, and points."[9]

"It is impossible to deny that he was an extraordinary man," a contemporary artist said of the architect, "a real creative genius. . . . He belonged to a race of human beings from another time for whom the awareness of higher order" took precedence over material things.[10]

Questions for Reflection

1. In his Letter to Artists, Pope St. John Paul II spoke of beauty as "an invitation to savor life."[11] Do you pause every day to appreciate the beauty around you? Beauty is present in many places—for example, nature, literature, the visual arts, and music. How do those places allow you to draw closer to God?

2. The Christian artist bears a special responsibility for helping others encounter beauty. Has there been a picture, sculpture, image, or piece of music that has caused you to become more aware of God's presence?

3. Think about the churches you have been in over the years. Which of these encouraged a spirit of prayer and drew you closer to God? How did the design, architecture, or setting inspire you?

CHAPTER TWO

Wife, Mother, Mystic

Barbe Acarie

Charism: Wisdom

Born February 1, 1566, in Paris, France
Died April 18, 1618, in Pontoise, France

I desire neither to live nor to die; I will only what God wills and nothing else.

—Barbe Acarie[12]

Born into a wealthy family in mid-sixteenth-century France, Barbe Avrillot quietly resisted the path laid out for her by her parents, particularly her status-conscious mother—marriage into a prominent, equally wealthy family. Her determined mother, suspecting correctly that her only daughter wanted to become a nun, took the direct approach. She set out to break Barbe's will by subjecting her to harsh treatment, presumably the sort she might expect in the penitential life of the convent. The teenager was not allowed to warm herself at the fire, for example, during the frigid winter of 1581 and, as a result, lost a toe to amputation when infection set in following a condition similar to frostbite.

In spite of her mother's treatment, Barbe chose to obey her parents and submitted without bitterness to the social whirl marked out for her. Precociously devout and centered on the will of God, she exhibited, even then, the intelligence, graciousness, and interior calm that led others to dub her, later in life, "La Belle Acarie."

She was sixteen and a beauty—with thick chestnut-colored hair and deep green eyes—when she married the devout, impetuous, and handsome twenty-two-year-old Pierre Acarie. Together they had six children, three of whom became nuns and at least one a priest (possibly two sons became priests—the record is unclear). Far from the monastic atmosphere that might be expected, the Acarie home was lively and affectionate, and the children arrived in rapid succession.

Between their third and the fourth children, however, Barbe's life took the turn that would bring her to prominence as one of the leaders of the remarkable Catholic revival that enveloped France well into the seventeenth century. She liked to read novels, a natural way to pass the time as she rocked her babies. One day Pierre picked up a book from her stack, flipped through some pages, and was disturbed by content that he considered too worldly. Mild enough by any standard, it was not spiritual. Pierre consulted a priest and, on his advice, took away the books and replaced them with devotional material.

Barbe always deferred cheerfully to Pierre, much as she had deferred to her parents, seeing this as a path to humility and to conforming herself to God's will. In this instance, she dutifully began reading the books he gave her. One day as she read, she came upon a phrase from St. Augustine's writing: "You are too greedy if God is not enough for you." In an instant, mysteriously, she felt herself transformed. She soon found herself entering into mystical union with God, marked by frequent ecstasies. These punctuated her days, causing her great embarrassment. Eventually, she learned to respond to the ecstasies in such a way that she could experience the presence of God while carrying on her normal life. She remained an engaged and happy wife and mother.

During these years, as Barbe was maturing in her faith, France was embroiled in the Wars of Religion that dominated the country in the late sixteenth century. Paris was under siege. In 1590, yet another horrific episode unfolded in the ongoing tit-for-tat mayhem. Famine set in as the Protestants, under Henry of Navarre, besieged the Catholic stronghold of Paris. Bones from the cemetery were ground up and added to flour to extend it, dogs and cats ended up in soup, and starvation was widespread. During the five months of the siege, Barbe spent herself in service to the sick and in distributing food to the hungry. When she discovered that her own mother-in-law had stuffed a large reserve of wheat into mattresses, she reproached her. If you insist on keeping it, she told her, "hide it where I can't find it, for if I do I shall certainly give it to the poor."[13]

The conservative Catholic League—a religious-political entity founded in 1576—led the defense of Paris, and the hotheaded Pierre was one of its premier members. He had already given a great deal of money to the cause and was so ardent on its behalf that his enemies nicknamed him "the Lackey of the League." And the League had enemies not only among Protestants but also among politically moderate Catholics who deplored the mutual slaughters that crippled France.

With the help of Spain, Paris was saved, but when Henry of Navarre became king a few years later (he converted to Catholicism to win the throne), he banished Pierre and other League leaders from Paris. Barbe, who apparently had not been involved in Pierre's political activity, rose to the challenge. Even as creditors stripped the furniture from their house and seized their home, she went to court and conducted the negotiations that ultimately saved their house and their wealth and obtained Pierre's pardon. Even the king was impressed.

As her reputation for sanctity grew, not only the poor but also saints began beating a path to her door—Sts. Francis de Sales and Vincent de Paul, for example, knew and praised her. Other luminaries as well as ordinary people seeking spiritual advice gathered at their home. For fifteen years, it became a kind of salon for the discussion, activities, and prayer that were the foundation of the burgeoning Catholic revival.[14]

Her humility—she actively discouraged curiosity about her mystical life—undergirded her charism for wisdom, and it was said that all of Paris sought her advice. She was given the ability to discern the interior spiritual state or needs of others. The provincial of the Jesuits, for example, said that when he consulted her, "What she told me was known to God alone. She showed me all the consequences which [my] business might entail, and nothing could have been truer."[15] For his part, Pierre found his home life challenging, and he sometimes turned people away when they came to the door or peppered guests with prying questions or became moody and petulant. But Barbe's love for him and joyful attentiveness to him never flagged during the thirty-one years of their marriage.

Barbe carried on her intense level of activity in spite of severe physical challenges. On her return from visiting Pierre when he was in exile—she was not yet thirty—she fell from her horse and was dragged a distance, breaking her hip. The repair was done poorly, and the hip was broken and reset; however, not long after, she fell and broke her thigh—twice. She walked with a cane, was unable to stand for long periods, and also suffered several severe illnesses. In the midst of her suffering, she achieved one of the most remarkable accomplishments of her life.

In 1601, she had a vision in which Teresa of Ávila appeared to her and asked her to introduce the Carmelite reform—the

Discalced Carmelites cofounded by Sts. Teresa and John of the Cross—into France. Barbe consulted her spiritual advisors and judging that the time was not right, they put the idea on the back burner. But when another vision followed in 1602, they gave the go-ahead and she began the arduous, politically complicated process of bringing several of Teresa's Spanish nuns into France to establish the order there. Barbe also acted as project manager for the construction of their convent, and she personally helped choose and form the women who became the first French novices, an unusual role for a laywoman. Throughout, she worked closely with her spiritual advisors but, said a colleague at the time, "She was the one at the helm."[16] Her daughters eventually became Carmelite nuns, and when Pierre died in 1613, Barbe entered the Carmelite foundation at Amiens as a lay sister, taking the name Marie of the Incarnation.

She lived another four years, and on her death, one of her sons promoted her cause for canonization. An associate, during the canonization process, said of her that "all who approached her were impressed by her genuine spirituality, and felt that in talking with her they were coming very close to God Himself."[17] She was beatified in 1791 under her religious name, Marie of the Incarnation, but her vocation was first of all as a laywoman who wholeheartedly embraced her roles as wife and mother. She found holiness there. As one of her admirers wrote, "Her message consisted of a sentence from the gospel, the full sense of which only mystics realize: "The Kingdom of God is within you."[18]

Questions for Reflection

1. Barbe chose to follow her parents' plan for her life and she married, a decision that bore great fruit. How do you make major life decisions? Have you ever followed a path that seemed right, even if difficult? How have your major life choices impacted your life?

2. The Wars of Religion wreaked havoc in France, but holy men and women looked to God to put themselves at the service of renewal. In our polarizing era, what can you do to bring light and reconciliation to your relationships? How can you help to bring about healing in your own corner of the Church and the world?

3. Barbe's charism for wisdom was extraordinary, but wisdom is a gift of the Holy Spirit available to every Christian. Do you actively pray for wisdom? How does this gift manifest itself in your life?

CHAPTER THREE

Mary of Ant Town
Satoko Kitahara

◆

Charism: Voluntary Poverty

Born August 22, 1929, in Tokyo, Japan
Died January 23, 1958, in Tokyo, Japan
Declared Venerable January 22, 2015

I had thought I was a great Christian because I condescended to dole out some free time, helping Ants [destitute] children with their homework! . . . It hit me now. There was only one way to help those ragpicker children: become a ragpicker like them!
—Satoko Kitahara[19]

By the time Satoko Kitahara was twenty, she had endured the fire bombing of Tokyo—the single most destructive bombing raid of World War II, contracted tuberculosis, lost two siblings to the war, and had questions about the meaning of life that neither her Shinto faith nor her Samurai heritage could answer.

Satoko grew up in a comfortable suburb of Tokyo—her mother was from a wealthy family, and her father was a university professor descended from a long line of Shinto priests. The family also owned a shoe business. Satoko's education reflected the expectations for Japanese women of the time. Women should learn European languages, one educator said, so that "they would be able to put their husbands' books back in the bookcase right side up after they had dusted them off."[20] Satoko was charming and intelligent, played classical piano, and in general embodied the spirit of Japanese womanhood.

And then came the war.

Although only fifteen, Satoko worked at the Nakajima aircraft factory, one of the many targets of American bombing runs. She survived a direct hit to the factory, telling a fellow worker, "If I am to die, let me die with a friend."[21] She did nearly die of tuberculosis toward the end of the war, but she recovered and, after Japan's surrender, found herself at loose ends and deeply disillusioned with life. Looking for a way to make herself useful, she entered pharmaceutical college.

But life took an unexpected turn.

While in nearby Yokohama to visit a friend, she passed by Sacred Heart Church and, on impulse, entered. There she came upon a statue of Our Lady of Lourdes—by all accounts, a statue of poor quality. This was the first time she had seen an image of Mary, however, and she gazed at it, "sensing the presence of a very attractive force that I could not explain."[22] Not long after, she met a fellow student whose joy was so compelling that Satoko asked her the source of her joy. The student told her she'd begun going to the same church where Satoko had encountered the statue of Mary.

Satoko's niece attended a school run by Mercedarian nuns, and Satoko also began to talk with them about the Catholic faith. She was intrigued when one of the nuns referred to God's "Providence," a concept that was new to her and very different from the concept of fate with which she was familiar. The sisters responded to her interest by instructing her in the essentials of Christian faith. Soon Satoko began attending Mass. "I had always experienced a vague but strong yearning for the Pure,"[23] she said, and having found the answer to her yearning in the person of Jesus Christ, she was baptized on October 30, 1949. She took the name Mary as her Confirmation name and Elizabeth as her baptismal name, inspired by St. Elizabeth of Hungary's service to the poor. "From when I was baptized I experienced a desire, amounting almost to a necessity, to serve," she said, "which seemed to be a natural accompaniment to being a follower of Christ."[24]

It would be some time, however, before her path of service became clear. She wanted to join the Mercedarian order and was accepted, but her tuberculosis flared up and prevented her from entering. Uncertain of her next steps, she happened to meet Brother Zeno Zebrowski, a Polish Franciscan brother who had come to Japan with St. Maximilian Kolbe and had remained there, serving the poor, when Kolbe returned to Poland.

Well-known and loved throughout Japan for his work on behalf of the destitute, Brother Zeno introduced Satoko to the reality of the homeless, broken, and hungry people who filled the devastated streets of Tokyo after the war. Specifically, he introduced her to the ragpickers who lived in what was known as "Ant Town," a squalid settlement of those who were homeless who made their living sorting through Tokyo's garbage, collecting and selling reusable materials. The encampment was known as Ant Town because the residents were as busy as ants.

Satoko felt herself drawn to the many children in Ant Town and began to teach and play with them, visiting them daily. She also began to sort through and sell garbage, overcoming her instinctive loathing for the dirty work. All this came at a steep price for the fastidious Satoko, who was loved by the children of Ant Town but viewed with suspicion by the unofficial Ant Town leaders—a tough ex-criminal, Motomu Ozawa, and a cynic named Toru Matsui. She had begun to win their respect when her tuberculosis flared up and she had to retreat to the mountains for many months to recuperate.

On her return, others had taken her place working with the children and she was again refused entrance into the Mercedarian order. Her parents wanted her to marry—but Satoko chose instead to live in celibacy and poverty. Once again, Satoko's health worsened and she was confined to bed. She prayed a novena, looking for a way forward, but feeling like a failure, she fell into a period of deep darkness.

Around this time, Motomu Ozawa visited her and announced he was going to be baptized. He told her that if God had inspired her to help the people of Ant Town, then he wanted to know that God too. Both he and Toru Matsui were baptized in October 1952. At his baptism, Matsui took the name Joseph. He said he chose it because Joseph had protected Mary, and he intended to protect Satoko, the Mary of Ant Town.

Soon after, in response to her unwavering determination to live in Ant Town, the two leaders prepared a small room for her there in a shed. Her doctor wisely supported the move—Satoko by now was in serious condition and he felt that the psychological boost would help restore her. He was right. She moved in, and although she was unable to do any strenuous work, she visited the elderly, did secretarial work for the town, wrote a pamphlet about the value of collecting and recycling garbage, and spent an increasing amount of time in prayer and intercession. Her prayer helped turn the tide when the Tokyo City government, considering Ant Town an eyesore, tried to get rid of the settlement in order to build a park.

As her illness progressed, she prayed from her bed within sight of a three-foot-tall statue of Our Lady of Lourdes, placed there for her by Ozawa and Matsui. Toward the end of her life, Satoko told her niece that there is nothing to fear—all that is good can be found in Catholicism. On January 23, 1958, after taking a sip of water that her mother offered her, Satoko said, "How good it is," and she died. She was twenty-eight years old.

Not long after Satoko's death, a major Japanese film company released a movie about her life, and in 1990, a prestigious magazine named her as one of the fifty most influential Japanese women of the twentieth century.

Questions for Reflection

1. Satoko, Ozawa, and Matsui formed an unlikely alliance—the privileged Satoko teaming up with the rough and initially unbelieving leaders of Ant Town. How do you feel about working for a cause with people who don't share your beliefs and values? Do you look for those opportunities? How do you relate to others in those situations?

2. It was important to Satoko not only to serve the poor but also to become one of them. Do you know—or know of—anyone who has a similar charism for voluntary poverty? In what ways is voluntary poverty effective in witnessing to the power of the gospel?

3. Satoko's baptism didn't suddenly provide all the answers to how she would live or what she should do next. Are you as determined to discover and pursue the charisms that God has given you? If not, what's stopping you?

CHAPTER FOUR

Apostle of Mercy and Justice
Frédéric Ozanam

Charisms: Mercy and Knowledge

Born April 23, 1813, in Milan, Italy
Died September 8, 1853, in Marseille, France
Beatified August 22, 1997

Our faith is weak because we cannot see God. But we can see the poor, and we can put our finger in their wounds, and see the marks of the crown of thorns.

—Frédéric Ozanam[25]

When Frédéric Ozanam arrived in Paris in 1831 to study law, it was not the beloved City of Light familiar to tourists today. "Paris disgusts me," he wrote in a letter to a friend. This was the Paris of Victor Hugo's *Les Miserables*—the filthy, dangerous, overcrowded tinderbox that Hugo immortalized in his book a few years later.

Ozanam's dissatisfaction stemmed not only from his firsthand exposure to the extreme poverty but also from his exposure to the rampant hostility to the Catholic Church evident everywhere. "There is no life, no faith, no love," he said, and he might have added, because he felt the loss keenly, there was no family life for him there.[26] He had left his parents and two siblings back in Lyon, and alone in the big city at the age of eighteen, he missed them.

Frédéric was in Paris, however, in obedience to his father, who insisted he become a lawyer—a more secure career path than that offered by the study of literature, Frédéric's own preference. Nevertheless, he threw himself into his studies, soon adding to these his determined efforts to defend the faith on all fronts, including in the classroom where professors routinely mocked it. Once, when a professor derided Christianity in a lecture, Ozanam wrote a rebuttal and asked the professor to read it to the students at the next class meeting. The professor agreed but didn't follow through although Frédéric confronted him twice. Ozanam persisted, gathered signatures in protest, and the professor finally complied and even apologized for his comments.

Under the guidance of a sympathetic former professor, Frédéric and some other students started a Catholic discussion group in which he rose to the top as "first among equals," as a friend later described him. "He has the sacred fire," another friend said of him. "There is such an air of interior conviction in this man, that without the appearance of doing so, he convinces and moves you."[27]

It was a time of revolution in France—riots, bloodshed, and bitter politics divided the country, and the Church was under siege, perceived by some as irrelevant and by others as too closely allied with a conservative point of view and too distant from the poor. Entering into the fray, the student group held lively, freewheeling discussions and debates, open to all and attracting large crowds. At one of these meetings, when the topic centered on Christianity's role in history, someone in the crowd called out, "What is your church doing now? What is she doing for the poor of Paris? Show us your works and we will believe."[28]

In response, Frédéric and his friends began going to the slums, offering whatever relief they could, from food to firewood to any money they could spare. They made it a point to get to know the poor, spending time with them. "Social welfare reform is to be learned not in books or from a public platform," he said, "but in climbing the stairs to a poor man's garret, sitting by his bedside, feeling the same cold that pierces him, sharing the secrets of his lonely heart and troubled mind."[29]

The group placed itself under the patronage of St. Vincent de Paul, the French apostle of charity, and focused both on serving the poor and encouraging the spiritual life of its members. It became known as the Society of St. Vincent de Paul, and within a few years, there were twenty-five conferences (chapters) in Paris; by Ozanam's death there were fifteen thousand members in eighteen countries. Ozanam's charism of mercy found full expression here, and though he never claimed to be the Society's founder—there were five or so others involved at the start—the title is rightly his. He threw himself into the laity-led charitable initiative right up until his death and is largely responsible for its wide acceptance, rapid expansion, and international presence today.

In the midst of this whirlwind of activity—he also wrote extensively and studied foreign languages in his spare time—Frédéric received a bachelor's degree in law, a bachelor's degree in arts, and, in 1836, a doctorate in law. He returned to Lyon to practice law and was soon appointed to the law faculty at the University of Lyon. Shortly after his return, his father died. Ozanam had revered him, describing him as his guardian angel and a wellspring of sound advice, and he now assumed responsibility for the care of his mother, whom he also revered. "Happy the man to whom God has given a holy mother," he wrote to a friend on her death in early 1840.[30]

With his mother's passing and unhappy as a lawyer, Frédéric now felt at loose ends in Lyon. He had pursued his interest in literature alongside his other activities, and while in Lyon had produced a groundbreaking thesis on the poet Dante. The Sorbonne granted him a doctorate in literature and in 1841 asked him to join the faculty in Paris as a professor of literature. He was only twenty-seven years old at this point, but his extraordinary intellectual gifts were undeniable and were equally as strong as his love for his Catholic faith.

His students revered him—his scholarship, sense of humor, faith, and compassion were all at the fore in his classroom. He was particularly attentive to the students who seemed to struggle. On one occasion, for example, he pulled aside the lowest-ranking student and walked him carefully through all the details of the class. The student, accustomed to being scorned by his professors and classmates, sent a note of thanks the next day. He finished the school year with the "first prize in general excellence" and went on to become a professor himself.[31]

In the midst of these challenging years, Frédéric had left the question of his state in life unsettled. He considered the priesthood but decided against it, immersed as he was in a full life as a layman. A priest who was a longtime friend and spiritual guide urged him to marry and acted as a matchmaker, setting up a visit between Frédéric and the warmhearted, intelligent Amélie Soulacroix. They were married on June 23, 1841, and—in a gesture that reveals something of the depth of their union—throughout their marriage, Frédéric brought her a bouquet of flowers on the twenty-third day of every month. In 1845, Amélie gave birth to their daughter, Marie, a blessing that Frédéric considered perhaps the greatest of his life.

Ozanam had never been physically robust but he contracted tuberculosis, and under the years of intense labor, his health finally broke in 1846. He took a year off from teaching, and he and his family traveled through Italy where he worked to foster the St. Vincent de Paul Society while continuing his literary research and trying to rest. Meanwhile, across Europe, the Revolutions of 1848 loomed—events that Ozanam in some ways anticipated. He had long advocated not only for active charity but also for social justice as intrinsic to the dignity of humanity, especially of the poor and the workers on the margins of society. "It is a struggle between those who have nothing," he wrote, "and those who have too much,"—promising a "violent clash of luxury and poverty."[32] In spite of his health, he served briefly in the National Guard in Paris during the 1848 uprising, but by 1852 he was on the brink of complete collapse.

He gave up his position at the Sorbonne and once again headed to Italy with his family, hoping to recover his health. When death appeared inevitable, the family returned to France, and he died in the port city of Marseille. He struggled, at the end, not only with leaving his family behind but also with intense regret over leaving his scholarship unfinished. But he had always strived, he said, to abandon himself to the will of God. "We are here to accomplish the will of Providence," he wrote, and when the end came, he made "these sacrifices when Providence" required them—"with love and joy."[33]

Frédéric Ozanam was beatified by Pope St. John Paul II in 1997.

Questions for Reflection

1. One of the most striking aspects of Frédéric Ozanam's work with the poor was his insistence on spending time with those in need. How can you show your concern and offer encouragement to those in need around you?

2. Ozanam had an extraordinary charism of knowledge, but he was humble about his gifts. What gifts has God given you? How can you put them to use for the good of others?

3. Ozanam studied law in obedience to his father's wishes, despite his inclination for literature. It was in this context that he defended his faith in an often hostile environment. Have you had the experience of defending your faith in a disapproving environment? How did this impact you and those around you?

CHAPTER FIVE

Love beyond Borders

Georges and Pauline Vanier

Georges-Philéas Vanier

Charism: Diplomacy

Born April 23, 1888, in Montreal, Canada
Died March 5, 1967, in Ottawa, Canada

I ask you to open your eyes to human suffering, to direct your hearts to those who have not the strength to ask for help. Let us go to them. They have already been waiting too long.
—Georges Vanier[34]

Nine days after the German army invaded Poland on September 1, 1939, Canada declared war on Germany, joining Britain, France, Australia, New Zealand, and South Africa in the opening days of World War II. The conflagration spread quickly to France, where Georges Vanier, a career diplomat, had recently taken up his post as minister in the Canadian embassy. By the spring of 1940, the Germans were on the outskirts of Paris, and the evacuation of the city—where Georges worked and the Vaniers lived—was underway. Georges sent his wife, Pauline, and their four children ahead on their own perilous escape while he stayed behind in Paris to oversee the evacuation of Canadian nationals and others.

That he stayed at his post, barely escaping to England, would have surprised no one. His courage and his commitment to those in his care had been severely tested twenty years earlier when he led his battalion in battle during the bloody closing days of World War I. He was shot in the stomach, and an explosion shattered his right leg, leading to a full amputation of that leg, which left him in pain for the rest of his life. He refused to be evacuated to Canada, however, as long as his fellow Canadians continued to fight. The government awarded him the Military Cross and the Distinguished Service Order in recognition of his bravery and leadership.

On his return to Montreal at the end of World War I, Georges married the lively Pauline Archer, whose social skills and extroverted personality complemented his more reserved personality and his inclination, as a lawyer, to step back and examine facts. A devout Catholic, she set the tone for their marriage several days before the wedding when she wrote to the equally devout Georges:

> You and I are going upward hand and hand toward the Light, because God is drawing us to Himself. Our ambition must be to always set our sights on this summit. Nothing else matters. We mustn't forget that we were created for Him, and we must always show this with our lives. It will be our particular form of the apostolate.[35]

She proved to be an asset to his diplomatic work and was at his side, along with their growing family, as his various appointments took him abroad. Initially they traveled to Geneva, where he served as Canada's military representative to the League of Nations, and then to London, where he served with the Canadian High Commission—the consular's office—from 1931 to 1938.

When he was posted to Paris in 1939, war was already in the air. As France fell and Hitler installed the Vichy puppet regime—headquartered in Vichy, France—Georges warned that treachery would follow. He urged support for General Charles de Gaulle and his efforts to recruit a free French army to continue the fight, but he was ignored.[36] Sent back to Canada, he was shocked that most people there were indifferent to the war and to his pleas that the country take in more refugees, particularly Jews. When his warnings about the nature of the Vichy regime proved true, however, Georges was named the Canadian Minister to the Governments in Exile and left for London in early 1943. Pauline followed shortly after.

Six months later, as Germany's losses mounted, Georges joined de Gaulle in Algeria as Canadian representative to de Gaulle's provisional French government. And when the Allies liberated Paris on August 25, 1944, Georges was named Canadian ambassador to France. The position required that he travel to Buchenwald Concentration Camp shortly after the Allies freed it in April 1945. The camp still held twenty thousand prisoners, including children, and he was there to investigate the fate of interned Canadian citizens. In a scathing report for the Canadian government, Georges described the camp as "revolting." Commenting on the horrors perpetrated by the jailers, he said:

> One is forced to the conviction that those who did these horrible things saw nothing wrong in them; perhaps they were actually proud of their efficiency in producing death. . . . Though they have a veneer of Christianity, deep down they must still be barbarians—in saying this one is unfair to the barbarian because there is a scientific refinement about these horrors which barbarians . . . , living in a primitive state, could not invent.[37]

Pauline joined him in Paris. Named as a Red Cross representative, she threw herself into the work of resettling refugees and arranging care for the returning prisoners of war and the skeletal victims of the concentration camps as they arrived at Paris's train stations. Two of the Vaniers' older children had spent much of the war in England: Jean, who would go on to found L'Arche, the international community serving people with intellectual challenges, and Thérèse, who would become a medical doctor and eventually bring L'Arche to England. Three of the children remained in Montreal during the war, including the youngest, Michel, who was now four years old. To Georges and Pauline's relief, the family was soon reunited in France.

Georges continued to serve postwar efforts in Europe until he retired in 1953. He and Pauline returned to Canada where Georges found himself at loose ends—no surprise, given his penchant for hard work. He served on various corporate boards, worked with a center for homeless men, and he and Pauline traveled regularly to Europe. But it wasn't enough.

When he was seventy-one, Georges found himself back in action when he was appointed governor-general of Canada in 1959. Although largely a ceremonial position, it was a high-profile honor and involved meetings, speeches, negotiations, and travel across the vast country. His governorship saw separatists in Quebec, a predominantly French-speaking province, begin agitating for Quebec's secession from Canada. In the face of violence and terrorist incidents, Georges stood firmly for Canadian unity. He died in office in 1967, shortly after attending Mass in the chapel he and Pauline had installed in their government residence.

Georges' charism for diplomacy might seem a natural fit based on his personality, but it demanded continual development. In a book Jean Vanier wrote tracing his father's spiritual sources—*In Weakness, Strength*—he said that his father was a man of "exceptional courage," especially in the face of the unrelenting physical pain that increasingly left him exhausted.

He showed astonishing self-control and this in turn required
great effort on his part.... His instincts were to become angry
or exasperated easily, but very rarely did he allow such reactions
to be visible externally. And on the very few occasions when
he did show even so much as a gesture of impatience he would
profoundly and sincerely apologize afterwards.[38]

His dry "sense of humor, his love of the ridiculous" undoubt-
edly served him well in his diplomatic work, as did his ability to
make fun of himself and of his limited mobility. Once, a friend
chastised Georges for accepting the post of governor-general
at his "advanced" age. "You've already got one foot in the
grave!" the friend said. "I know," Georges replied, "but after
all, it's been there for 41 years!"

His natural gifts notwithstanding, Georges' lifelong career
in diplomacy flowed primarily from his ever-deepening faith.
Prayer did not come easily to him, but he persevered and gradually felt drawn more deeply into the presence of God. "I trust
in the mercy of Jesus and the direction of the Holy Spirit," he
wrote, and took as his motto as governor-general, "May God's
will be done."[39]

A Catholic and a diplomat to the end, he served people of
all faiths and no faith, respecting them regardless. In doing so,
he communicated his own faith. As Jean Vanier wrote,

He spoke very little in public about his faith in God. Rather it
was by other means, by the warm feeling of good will he seemed
to radiate, by his profound and extraordinary appreciation

of others, by the serenity of his bearing perhaps—in all these ways he transmitted a sense of the presence of God to others.[40]

Questions for Reflection

1. A charism for diplomacy is a specific gift, but we're all called to treat others with respect and tact. How do you handle difficult people or conversations? Are you able to turn to prayer during those times? What can you learn from Georges and the self-control that he cultivated?

2. Georges demonstrated that old age is no barrier to a life of service. How can older Catholics continue to exercise their charisms in service to others? What graces can older Catholics bring to the Church and to younger Catholics?

3. Georges didn't let the loss of his leg hinder his life of service. How can his example encourage you to overcome obstacles and serve from the place where you find yourself? In what ways can your own challenges help you to connect with and serve others?

Pauline Vanier

◈

Charism: Mercy

Born March 28, 1898, in Montreal, Canada
Died March 23, 1991, in Trosly-Breuil, France

The true Christian spirit looks upon all spiritual values, of whatever source, as part of the divine treasure entrusted to mankind by the Creator. . . . Faith, far from being outmoded or old-fashioned, imparts a beauty, a richness, and a radiance that can be found in no other source.

—Pauline Vanier[41]

Georges and Pauline Vanier had been married for seventeen years when they moved to Paris in the days immediately preceding World War II. The marriage, though happy, had been tested. The incessant travel, their limited finances, the need to entertain often and elegantly on behalf of Georges' work as a diplomat, the birth of three children in six years followed by a threatened miscarriage of the fourth in 1928—these took their toll on the couple, but especially on Pauline. After she had safely delivered their fourth child—Jean—she had a breakdown and ended up in the hospital.

Throughout her life, Pauline suffered from anxiety and occasional bouts of depression. But her mother, who had been an orphan and was also subject to anxiety, had passed on to her daughter a deep sense of trust in God. This became Pauline's anchor.

Her strong faith coupled with her drive to reach out and help people gave her a firm sense of purpose as the years went on. She cultivated her inner life with the help of several spiritual advisors, and in 1938, she and Georges began attending daily Mass. They decided also to spend a half hour in prayer every day, a practice each continued for the rest of their lives.

Pauline's serene assurance of God's love and mercy helped Georges leave behind his rigid approach to faith—initially, he received Communion only a couple of times a year, for example, out of a sense of unworthiness and fear of sin. Georges found it hard to believe, she said later in life, that she could be out dancing and drinking champagne at a diplomatic function and receive Communion the next day. Nevertheless, Pauline's growth in faith was a lifelong process as she sought internal peace and a sense of direction when life threw her a curve.

On the other hand, her interest in people seemed effortless and was a hallmark of her vivacious personality. The only child of a superior court judge, she grew up in Montreal among the wealthy and elite, educated by a series of governesses and completely at ease in social settings. She wanted more from life, however, and secretly completed a nursing program during World War I. To her parent's dismay, she then served in a military hospital for the duration of the war. She had considered becoming a nun, but when she met Georges, she knew she had met her match—a man who shared her Catholic faith and her inclination to serve.

Their life in the diplomatic corps would take them into harrowing situations, but her courage and instinct to help others never failed. When she and her children were escaping by car from Paris during World War II, for example, the road was jammed with evacuees and under heavy bombardment. A German plane crashed on the roadside ahead of them, but her first thought was for the pilot. She jumped out of the car, hoping to rescue him, but the plane went up in flames.

As Red Cross representative in Paris after the war, while Georges served as Canada's ambassador to France, she wrote countless letters to Canada soliciting funds and basic necessities and answering the letters that piled up from the French who were desperate for help. Every day she went to a repatriation center where concentration camp victims arrived in droves. "This is truly the bursting out of evil in all its horror," she wrote. "Most of them were in a frightful physical condition, so thin and weak that they could hardly walk; their shaven heads and diaphanous faces are pathetic."[42]

The war years weighed heavily on Pauline for another reason—the long separation from her children. Her separation from Michel was especially grueling. He was only two when she left him in the care of her mother, and she wouldn't see him again until he was four.

Deeper Mercy

When Georges and Pauline returned to Canada in 1953, they could easily have settled into well-earned retirement. Pauline had endured breast cancer shortly before and had had a complete mastectomy. Her full recovery notwithstanding, it was one more challenge in a lifetime of challenges. On the other hand, their son Georges, who had entered the Trappist monastery in Oka, Canada, had been ordained a priest. "The moment of the consecration was to me the most extraordinary instant of my life," she wrote in a letter to a friend. "To think that this child of mine had the power to bring our Creator down on the altar there for us to receive, how mysterious and how wonderful."[43]

To the relief of Georges senior, at least, retirement was off the table. When he accepted the post of governor-general of Canada, together they accepted a pace of travel and hospitality that rivaled their European years. It came to an abrupt halt in 1967 with Georges' sudden death. Pauline was almost seventy and could not have guessed that she had nearly twenty-four years as a widow ahead of her. She could also not have guessed that she would spend them in Trosly, France, at L'Arche, as the honorary grandmother to the mentally disabled and those who cared for them.

Initially, the idea was not entirely welcome.

She had been on retreat and one day, at Mass, the Gospel reading was that of the rich young man who asks Jesus what he must do to be saved. Jesus tells him to go, sell what he has, and follow him. The idea of moving to L'Arche had occurred to Pauline during the years since Georges' death, but the commitment—she was by now seventy-three—seemed over-whelming. And although she mingled easily with everyone, the "everyones" in her life had been weighted over the years toward such prominent figures as Winston Churchill and Car-dinal Angelo Roncalli, the future Pope John XXIII and papal nuncio to Paris after the war.

At L'Arche she would be surrounded by young, idealistic caregivers trying to find their way in life, over 200 mentally and physically challenged adults in need of affection and support, and a steady stream of guests from around the world eager to learn more about this new movement. Her accommodations would be spartan, at least at first, and would never reach the level of comfort she had enjoyed in various diplomatic post-ings and official government housing.

Pauline said yes anyway, sold or gave away many of her possessions and, a month short of her seventy-fourth birthday, moved to Trosly. Her charism for mercy, evident throughout her life, came into full focus during these years, but as she had suspected, it wasn't easy. L'Arche was still in its early days and, as Jean Vanier said years later, he was inexperienced, idealistic, and made mistakes as a leader. "The community was growing rather wildly without much vision or common reflection," he wrote.[44] Further, he was away much of the time, helping to establish similar communities or leading retreats around the world. Pauline had expected to see her son fairly often, but for the most part, she was denied that consolation.

She called her new life "the school of L'Arche" with its inevitable stripping away "day by day of what I was and still am."[45] The disabled who lived there—known as core members—carried wounds from years of rejection and loneliness, but she quickly saw that the young people who arrived to work were suffering too. "I have had a chance to know this," she wrote, soon after moving in, "as many of them have already come to see me and have poured their heart out; this seems to be my job—a recipient of other people's suffering. I am trying very hard to listen well and to give some joy."[46]

Listening and giving joy continued to be her job for the next two decades as she made herself available to everyone—helpers, core members, and guests—and visited the group homes dotting the town, welcomed the core members who visited her or helped her out at home (often just wandering in without knocking), threw parties and arranged prayer meetings in her house for the assistants, and in general became the grandmother of L'Arche. As advanced age slowed her down, she found herself dealing with old anxieties and a feeling of uselessness, but she struggled to maintain a spirit of abandonment to God and the life she had chosen. She died after surgery for newly diagnosed colon cancer a few days before her ninety-third birthday and is buried beside Georges at the Citadel in Quebec City, Canada.

Georges had once said of her, in reference to their life together, "Pauline is the best half of the team."[47] She had said to him, in one of her annual letters to him on the anniversary of his war wound, "Living by your side is a great grace. . . . I thank you from the bottom of my heart."[48]

Their son Jean said of them both that together they "created between them a family spirit. . . . The warmth and forthrightness of my father linked with the vivacity and spontaneity of my mother never failed to bring out the best" in others.[49] Their cause for canonization as a married couple has been proposed and is under investigation.

Questions for Reflection

1. Pauline was frank about her struggles with anxiety and depression, allowing her spiritual advisors to help her. Do you turn to others for help when you struggle, or do you try to go it alone? How might the support of other Christians help you to handle your own struggles, whatever they may be?

2. Pauline left behind the privileges of her status when she went to live at L'Arche. What can her example teach you about flexibility and a readiness to answer God's call even in old age? Whether young or old, have you prayed for a willingness to serve in whatever capacity God asks?

3. Georges and Pauline, together, were a powerful force for the gospel. If you are married, how can their example help you and your spouse surrender, together, to God's call? If you are single, how can you help married couples to discover and use their charisms?

CHAPTER SIX

Beginning Again on Molokai

Joseph Dutton

Charism: Helps

Born April 27, 1843, in Stowe, Vermont
Died March 26, 1931, in Honolulu, Hawaii

I wish to guard you against having too high an estimate of the work here. Work performed with a good intention, to accomplish the will of the Almighty God, for his glory, is the same in one place as in another. One's Molokai can be anywhere.

—Joseph Dutton[50]

"I am ashamed to think that I am inclined to be jolly," Joseph Dutton said at the age of eighty-three. "My laugh is ready to burst out any minute."[51] The setting for Joseph's happiness was an unlikely one—the leper colony at Kalawao on the Kalaupapa peninsula of Molokai.

Beginning in 1865, the Hawaiian government confined victims of leprosy to the island, in a policy of forced segregation. Chosen for its remote and escape-proof nature, the island settlement was bordered by mountains, the ocean, and the steepest sea cliffs in the world.

Not that Joseph wanted to escape. He had come freely to help Fr. Damien De Veuster, who had labored there for thirteen years and had become a victim of the disease. "I've come to help, and I've come to stay," he told Fr. Damien when they first met. The priest was a "leper in the advanced stages," Dutton recalled forty years later of his first encounter with Fr. Damien at Molokai on July 29, 1886. Damien had begged his religious order, the Congregation of the Sacred Heart, to send him priests and brothers, but the order "had none to spare," Joseph said, "so he called me Brother."[52]

Fr. Damien, whose heroic work had transformed the squalid colony into a hospitable community, said that the arrival of Dutton eased his mind. Brother Joseph is "truly an exemplary self-devoting man. He will be our right hand," he wrote to a friend. "He is a true brother to me." Knowing, especially, that he could entrust to Joseph's care the many orphans at Molokai, Fr. Damien said, "I can die now."[53] He died almost three years after Joseph's arrival.

Brother Joseph remained on Molokai, in robust health, for nearly forty-five years. He never developed leprosy—now known as Hansen's disease—and could have abandoned the work and the people at any time. But he stayed, as promised, and he helped until shortly before his death in 1931, when he became ill and was transferred to a hospital in Honolulu.

Not many who knew Ira Barnes Dutton prior to his conversion to Brother Joseph would have predicted his self-sacrifice, including Joseph himself. In fact, he said, a graph of his life would map out as "45 years down and 45 years up."[54]

His family moved to Janesville, Wisconsin, when he was four, and he grew up as an Episcopalian. As an adult, he taught Sunday school and worked in a bookstore before joining the 13th Wisconsin Infantry Regiment during the Civil War. After the war, he married a woman who was unfaithful to him—something his friends had warned him about before the marriage. She left with another man and ran up debts in her husband's name.

Ira Dutton began to drink heavily—a barrel of whiskey a year for fifteen years, he once said. A functioning alcoholic, he managed to keep a string of steady jobs. His work included transferring the remains of dead soldiers to Arlington National Cemetery, overseeing a distillery in Alabama, working for the railroad in Tennessee, and settling war claims against the government. Apparently ashamed of his lifestyle—drunk by night, employed by day— he quit drinking in 1876 and never touched alcohol again. He divorced his wife in 1881 and became a Catholic in 1883. He took the name Joseph and began the upward swing that marked the remainder of his life.

After his conversion, Joseph looked for a way to make amends for what he called his "wild years." He never injured anyone but himself, he said of his hard-drinking lifestyle, but nevertheless he wanted to do penance for this and unnamed "sinful capers." He spent twenty months at the Trappist Abbey of Gethsemani in Kentucky but concluded this way of life wasn't for him. He traveled with a priest friend to New Orleans and there, in a monastery reading room, he happened upon a brief newspaper reference to Fr. Damien's work on Molokai. "I had never heard of him," he later said. "Why this suddenly impressed me with the certainty that I had found my real vocation, I have never tried to elucidate; but have acted as there was need to only go ahead, leaving the whys and wherefores to any who like such problems."[55] In fact, Dutton's gift for coming alongside others and helping them achieve their best for God had found a perfect match in the priest of Molokai.

Once on Molokai, he never looked back. He was a gifted administrator and businessman—an asset to the settlement that at its peak in 1890 housed 1,100 victims of the disease. But more than that, he had a heart for the work and for the victims consigned there. "I like them," he said simply of the people, and he felt that they liked him. He poured himself out for them, continuing to exercise his charism long after Fr. Damien's death. He learned how to clean and bandage wounds (he surpassed even the doctors at this), built cottages and latrines, gardened, ordered supplies, cleaned the homes of the sick, buried the dead, comforted the depressed and grieving, and, after Fr. Damien's death, took charge of a home for the many orphan boys on Molokai. He even developed a baseball team, supplying the young players with bright-colored uniforms, and carried on extensive correspondence with the outside world.

Joseph was "well-knit, slim, lithe, muscular,"[56] an observer said of him the day he disembarked at Molokai, and he never lost his military bearing over the nearly half century that followed. He joined the secular order of Franciscans in 1892, a worldwide association of laypeople who live simply, in the spirit of St. Francis of Assisi. When someone asked him late in life how he had reached such a vigorous old age, Dutton listed the usual reasons—no tobacco, alcohol, or coffee, lots of sunshine, fresh air, and exercise—but added that he didn't have any worries. This was in spite of the heavy load of responsibilities he carried. "I ceased worrying years ago," he said.[57]

Brother Joseph was extraordinarily calm, so much so that no one on Molokai ever heard him raise his voice or lose his temper. His self-discipline must have come at a cost, but he gave no indication that this was so. He had come to Molokai "not looking to hide, exactly,"[58] he once said, but looking to start again. When he began his new life, he did so with the wisdom, grace, and gratitude he had gained from his conversion and from his commitment to atone for his "45 years down." Shortly before he died, Joseph said that he had had a happy life on Molokai. He is buried on the island next to St. Philomena Church, built by victims of Hansen's disease in 1872.

When Brother Joseph died in 1931, he had outlived by decades two saints with whom he served on Molokai, Fr. Damien and Mother Marianne Cope, who worked there with her fellow Sisters of St. Francis. Fr. Damien was canonized in 2009, and Mother Marianne Cope was canonized in 2012. In 2015, the Diocese of Honolulu approved the statutes for the Joseph Dutton Guild, dedicated to investigating Brother Joseph's possible cause for canonization.

Questions for Reflection

1. Brother Joseph said that "one's Molokai can be anywhere"; what matters most is doing the will of God. In what ways can a seemingly ordinary life be extraordinary in regard to serving others?

2. According to Psalm 92, "The just . . . shall bear fruit even in old age." Brother Joseph served the Kalawao settlement well into his eighties. Do you know—or know of—older people who serve others wholeheartedly, continuing to bear fruit for the Lord? What difference does their witness make to the Church and to their own family and community?

3. As it does for many people, Brother Joseph's vocation unfolded gradually. Why do you think he was so certain that he was called to Molokai? How do you think he prepared himself to discern this call? What steps do you follow as you discern God's will for your life, whether in big or small matters?

CHAPTER SEVEN

Missionary without a Boat

Madeleine Delbrêl

◆

Charism: Hospitality

Born October 24, 1904, in Mussidan, France
Died October 13, 1964 in Ivry-sur-Seine, France
Declared Venerable January 27, 2018

To proclaim the Gospel in the language of the people with whom we are speaking is not enough. We have to proclaim the Gospel in the language of the Gospel, in the language of Jesus Christ. . . . And Christ's language is that of a good and brotherly heart.

—Madeleine Delbrêl[59]

In many ways, Madeleine Delbrêl's ministry of hospitality was ordinary—a one-on-one outreach to her neighbors in Ivry, a working-class suburb of Paris. In other ways, it was extraordinary: Ivry was the most communist and most atheist area of Paris—its residents full of hatred for Catholics and the Church. A former atheist herself, Madeleine brought with her a special sensitivity to the needs of her neighbors.

Madeleine grew up in a nonpracticing Catholic family and declared, at seventeen, that "God is dead. Long live death!" She was artistically inclined, designing and making her own clothes, cutting her hair fashionably short, and throwing parties with her friends under the theme "Life is meaningless." She was also intellectually curious and studied philosophy and art at the Sorbonne, reading aloud from her philosophical writings to her parents' nonreligious friends who were suitably impressed.

Madeleine became engaged to a fellow atheist, but after his own conversion, he broke the engagement in order to enter the Dominican Order. At the same time, her parents' marriage floundered, and Madeleine found herself, at the age of twenty, with more questions than answers.

Still, she had an instinct for friendship—she was warm, intelligent, a good listener and conversationalist, and always ready to defend her friends if need be. Late in 1924, Madeleine met some young people at a dance who turned out to be believing Catholics. Struck by their high-spirited freedom and intelligence, she began to consider the possibility that God might not be dead and that the Church might offer more than she had considered. Her new friends helped her on her quest, introducing her to a local priest, Abbé Lorenzo, who over the next several years guided her as she explored the faith. He led her through a study of the Old and New Testaments and taught her about the sacramental life of the Church.

At the same time, Madeleine began to pray. She later said that she found God by reading and reflecting. But it was when she prayed, she said, that God found *her* and that she discovered that "he is living reality . . . We can love him in the same way we love a person."[60]

She brought together a group of young women friends who read and discussed Scripture every week. Eventually they discerned a call to live as contemplatives in the midst of their world. She pursued her degree in social work, and then, when she was twenty-nine, a parish in Ivry offered her group a house, rent free, if they would live there among the poor. Madeleine and two friends took the parish up on the offer. Their home became, essentially, a house of compassionate hospitality. Neighbors freely came and went—an endless line of people seeking aid, consolation, food, and friendship.

Madeleine called Ivry "my school of applied faith." In an age when missionaries typically set sail for distant lands, she saw herself as a "missionary without a boat." She also worked closely with communists, coordinating help for refugees and the poor while living under Nazi occupation during World War II. In the process, she developed strong friendships with them, and at the end of the war, the communist mayor of Ivry invited her to be Minister of Social Services.

A prolific writer, Madeleine covered many political and spiritual topics in her books, including Marxist-Catholic relations. In *The Marxist City as Mission Territory*, she emphasized that Catholics need to love communists (a notion many Catholics resisted) and they could do so without embracing their ideology. Recognizing her apostolate, the Vatican invited her to join the commission composing the initial draft of the *Decree on the Apostolate of the Laity*.

One of her best-loved books, *We, the Ordinary People of the Streets*, captures her sense of the possibilities to be found on behalf of the gospel in ordinary life. She wrote,

There are some people whom God takes and sets apart.

There are others he leaves among the crowd, people he does not "withdraw from the world."

These are the people who have an ordinary job, an ordinary household, or an ordinary celibacy. People with ordinary sicknesses, and ordinary times of grieving. People with an ordinary house, and ordinary clothes. These are the people of ordinary life. The people we might meet on any street.

They love the door that opens onto the street, just as their brothers who are hidden from the world love the door that shuts behind them forever.

We, the ordinary people of the streets, believe with all our might that this street, this world, where God has placed us, is our place of holiness.[61]

Madeleine Delbrêl died suddenly at her desk of a brain hemorrhage at the age of sixty. She had lived her faith as "pure gift from God . . . right in the midst of everyday life."[62]

Questions for Reflection

1. We might be reluctant to practice hospitality because of past experiences. In his apostolic exhortation Rejoice and Be Glad, Pope Francis reminds us that "God is eternal newness. He impels us constantly to set out anew, to pass beyond what is familiar, to the fringes and beyond" (135). How can the Holy Spirit help you to be open to encountering others whose ways are different from yours?

2. Hospitality should be a key feature of Catholic parishes. The Second Vatican Council's Decree on the Apostolate of the Laity makes the point that "to cultivate good human relations, truly human values must be fostered, especially the art of living fraternally and cooperating with others and of striking up friendly conversation with them" (29). What steps can you take to reach out to others before and after Mass? What would it take for you to strike up a conversation with someone you don't know or someone who is alone?

3. Madeleine Delbrêl developed friendships and respected the freedom of people whose worldview was contrary to hers. The Decree on the Apostolate of the Laity adds that "it is imperative also that the freedom and dignity of the person being helped be respected with the utmost consideration" (8). How can you cooperate with people of goodwill to serve the poor and the needy in your neighborhood?

CHAPTER EIGHT

Nurses, the Happiest People

Hanna Chrzanowska

Charism: Leadership

Born October 7. 1902, in Warsaw, Poland
Died April 29. 1973, in Kraków, Poland

Let us not just think about fighting evil. . . . Can't we also shout about goodness?

—Hanna Chrzanowska[63]

Hanna Chrzanowska's hometown of Kraków had become something of a garrison town during World War I—military barracks and hospitals dotted the landscape. The war ended in 1918, but in Poland the Polish-Soviet War followed swiftly on its heels, and soldiers from both wars crowded Kraków's military hospitals. In 1920, in an effort to meet the overwhelming demand for hospital care, the Red Cross set up a two-week course to train volunteers to tend the wounded. Eighteen-year-old Hanna signed up and spent the summer preceding university studies doing gritty hands-on work in an army hospital. "To this day I can hear the screams of the young soldiers," she wrote decades later.[64]

Rather than deter her, the sobering experience left her more committed than ever to her chosen career—nursing. Even in the absence of adequate nursing schools in Poland, she remained adamant about her choice. An outstanding student with plenty of drive, she could easily have pursued a career as a physician, with its perceived higher status. But when asked about her choice years later, Hanna said that she never wanted to be a doctor. "Never in my life have I regretted that I am not a physician. Instinctively I knew that medicine was one profession and nursing something entirely different again . . . something higher."

She viewed nursing as a form of social action and said that nurses are "the happiest people, those most in love with their profession, most grateful for the gift of life."[65] As far as her own life went, her instinct proved true, and she went on to play an important role in establishing nursing as a licensed and respected profession in Poland.

Hanna's experience of childhood illness, hospital stays, and lifelong poor health helped focus her career goals on nursing, but the roots of her social activism can be found in her well-to-do but deeply philanthropic family. "I grew up in an atmosphere of service to one's neighbour . . . ; as if this were the most natural (and normal)" approach to life, she said.[66] Her maternal grandparents established a school for artisans and a health center for poor children in Warsaw. Her father, Ignacy, established literacy schools for the poor in Warsaw before becoming a revered professor of Polish literature at Kraków's Jagiellonian University. Her mother, Wanda, put her financial resources into the pediatric hospital established by her sister, Zofia Szlenkier—Hanna's Aunt Zofia.

Aunt Zofia, with her independent spirit, commitment to suffering children, and intellectual integrity, had a significant impact on Hanna. Zofia not only founded a hospital for children and served as its director but also went to the nursing school at St. Thomas' Hospital in London, convinced that she needed to reinforce her administrative work with medical expertise. She brought back to Poland an enlightened vision for hospital nursing and the skills to implement her vision—as well as the joy of having met the inspirational Florence Nightingale, founder of the nursing school at St. Thomas' Hospital.

Hanna absorbed all these influences, and though she entered Jagiellonian University as a humanities major, she viewed the position as a holding place until either Poland opened a nursing school or she could arrange to study abroad. When a professional nursing school opened in Warsaw in 1922, she enrolled, completing her degree in 1924 and shortly after qualifying as a registered nurse.

Her outstanding abilities were evident while she was still a student. Consequently, a few months before graduation, the school offered her a scholarship to study community nursing and public health in Paris. In return, she was to help establish community-based nursing in Kraków and run a community-oriented nursing program at the newly formed, professional-level Kraków School of Nursing. Although she was primarily interested in seeing Paris—the director said that when she presented the offer, "Hanna was dancing on the edge of her chair"[67]—she found the experience life-changing from a professional standpoint as well. Increasingly her interest was shifting from hospital-based health care, her original goal, to community-based care that served people in clinics, in schools, and in their homes.

During this period between World War I and World War II, Hanna's charism for leadership flourished. She taught at the Kraków nursing school for several years, established clinics for pregnant women and infants, studied school-based nursing in Belgium, helped set up a school-nurse system in Kraków, collaborated in forming the Polish Association of Professional Nurses, served as editor of the new Polish nurses journal, worked as assistant director of the Warsaw nursing school, and even wrote a couple of novels. She accomplished all this and more in spite of ongoing health problems that required her to occasionally step back from her work to recuperate.

This was an exciting period in Poland—it was functioning as an independent country for the first time in nearly 150 years—and Hanna was in the thick of it, in part because she was in the right place at the right time, as the government prioritized the development of high-quality universal health care. The new Kraków nursing school was incorporated into Jagiellonian University's medical school, while allowed to remain completely autonomous—a vote of confidence and a rare honor.

Light in the Darkness

Something other than professional development was stirring in Hanna. She was a successful, esteemed nurse and had a wide circle of friends and colleagues and a deep interest in the arts, particularly in music and literature, but her Catholic faith had largely been on the periphery of her life. Her friendship with a devout fellow nurse and editor, however, prompted her to rethink questions of faith. She never wrote about her growing belief, but she did take a trip to Italy with her father in 1939 and found there, especially in Assisi, new insight and depth of faith. She became a Benedictine oblate—a lay member of the Benedictine order—drawn by their motto, *ora et labora*, "pray and work." By the outbreak of World War II, she was known as a deeply committed Catholic.

Almost immediately after the German army marched into Poland on September 1, 1939, igniting World War II, Hanna's family faced the consequences. They were evicted from their university-owned apartment so that German officers could move in. Hanna's beloved Aunt Zofia and her cousin Andrew Chrzanowski died in the battle for Warsaw.

As a university professor, Hanna's father was among those arrested and deported to Sachsenhausen concentration camp in Germany as part of *Sonderaktion Krakau*, the Nazi initiative to eradicate intellectual life in Kraków. Because he was a retired professor, Ignacy didn't need to show up when the German's demanded that the teaching staff appear for a lecture on November 6, but his commitment to the university and his colleagues prompted him to do so. He was rounded up along with the others—the call to attend a lecture was a ruse—and died at Sachsenhausen three months later, succumbing to the brutal conditions. Astonishingly, Hanna and her mother went to Germany and were allowed into the camp to recover his body. In order to keep a low profile on the return journey, they had his body cremated and carried the ashes back to Kraków.

Bhodan, Hanna's brother and only sibling, was a reserve officer who was trapped, along with thousands of others, when the Soviets launched a surprise attack during a battle in late 1939. He was sent to a Soviet prisoner of war camp and was murdered, along with approximately 20,000 other Polish officers and intelligentsia, in the infamous massacre in the Katyn woods. The massacre took place in the spring of 1940 on the direct order of Joseph Stalin, but it was years before family members learned the fate of the prisoners. Buried in a mass grave, Bhodan's body was later among those identified when German troops stumbled upon the sites of the executions and opened the graves.

In the midst of these unfolding horrors, Hanna went to work. She joined the RGO, the main Polish wartime welfare group and, because of her excellent command of German, acted as a liaison between the RGO in Kraków and the German authorities. Hanna eventually took charge of coordinating all the nursing care for the displaced people who poured into the city, organized volunteers to help with the effort, and taught them basic nursing skills. She also addressed the spiritual and psychological needs of the traumatized refugees. She even set up a food bank for those suffering from malnutrition.

Hanna shielded Jewish children from the Germans, placing them in foster homes or other safe houses, helped hide allied soldiers caught behind enemy lines, and on one occasion hid some English soldiers in an infectious disease ward unlikely to be entered by the Germans. On another occasion, she volunteered for extra shifts in a neonatal unit of a hospital for a few months. She wanted to keep an eye on a German doctor on the ward to make sure he wasn't euthanizing Polish babies. She had an alias in the underground resistance, but it remains unknown, as does much of her clandestine activity during the war.

Against the Odds

When the war ended, Hanna worked for the United Nations Relief and Rehabilitation Administration (UNRRA) and lectured on community nursing at Kraków's school of nursing. The UNRRA awarded her and other Polish nurses scholarships to study community nursing in New York City. When she returned to Kraków a year later in 1947, the now-communist government had begun clamping down on people of faith. However, they couldn't ignore her expertise because more than one-third of Poland's medical personnel had died during the war.[68] Poland was now a Soviet client state: daily life was heavily regulated, the government spied on everyone, and Hanna's staunch Catholicism was seen as a threat.

In 1958, the government forced her retirement by shutting down the psychiatric hospital to which it had assigned her. Undaunted, and in spite of growing health problems, she was free to throw herself into a long-held dream: parish-based nursing care that would bring professional nurses into the homes of the chronically ill, the disabled, the housebound, and the elderly. That she succeeded in her determination to meet the needs of this underserved population is a testimony not only to her leadership skills but also to her perseverance.

The approach was novel, especially in a communist country—the government harassed her and in particular attempted to obstruct the group pilgrimages she planned for her patients and the retreats she developed and led for her nurses and the small army of volunteers who supported her work. It was novel too for the Church: not only the laity-led retreats, but also the parish-based and laity-led professional nursing provided by paid—not volunteer—nurses. Nevertheless, while novel, her vision was unfolding just as the Church was emphasizing the role of the laity and preparing for Vatican Council II.

As she struggled to bring her idea to life, help arrived from what proved to be, in the long run, a notable quarter: a friend suggested she get in touch with a young priest at St. Florian's parish, Fr. Karol Wojtyła. The priest—the future Pope St. John

Paul II—immediately took to her idea and put her in touch with Fr. Ferdinand Machay, a priest known for his social activism who would help her move forward. Fr. Wojtyła stayed in touch, however, and the two became friends. She took him with her on a typical home visit to thirty-five patients, and he understood, for the first time, the vast scale of the need. His continued support and the generous response, especially, of the Catholic laity helped parish-based nursing take root and flourish in Kraków.

Hanna's ill health was exacerbated over the years by growing sensitivities to drugs and disinfectants that could have kept her from visiting the sick. She ignored the severe allergic reactions she endured in hospitals and sickrooms, however, in favor of continuing to meet face-to-face with those in poor health. She could not ignore the diagnosis of cancer, however, and in spite of several surgeries that prolonged her life, she died on April 29, 1973.

Cardinal Wojtyła visited her shortly before her death. In a gesture that captures his compassion for the sick as well as his esteem for Hanna, before leaving he rolled up his sleeves and helped her aide reposition the disoriented Hanna so that she was in a more comfortable position.[69] He was the main celebrant at her funeral Mass. At the cemetery, when the time came for him to chant the somewhat somber Salve Regina, he broke with tradition and sang, instead, the Magnificat, Mary's joyful hymn of praise.

"Let your reward be the Lord himself," Cardinal Wojtyła said at her burial, and "let the radiance of your service . . .

linger . . . and constantly teach us how to serve Christ in our neighbors."[70]

Hanna Chrzanowska was beatified by Pope Francis on April 28, 2018.

Questions for Reflection

1. Hanna's family provided strong witness to the importance of personal and professional excellence as well as generosity of spirit. Do you value these traits in your own life? How? Do you think they are an important part of Catholic history and witness?

2. Hanna was single-minded about the importance of healthcare, but she was also prudent, as demonstrated by the way she handled her work under the Nazi and Communist regimes in power. What can you learn from her about the prudent and patient pursuit of your own goals, either personal or professional?

CHAPTER NINE

To the Heights
Pier Giorgio Frassati

Charism: Mercy

Born April 6, 1901, in Turin, Italy
Died July 4, 1925, in Turin, Italy

*No human being should ever be abandoned, whatever his race
or religion; charity should surmount all barriers.*
—Pier Giorgio Frassati[71]

As twenty-four-year-old Pier Giorgio lay sick in his bed in the family home in Turin, Italy, his grandmother lay dying a few doors down. All eyes were on the grandmother, however, and no one noticed the creeping paralysis that was slowly claiming Pier Giorgio. On the contrary, his mother chided him: "It seems impossible that whenever you are needed you are never there," she said. To a friend who stopped by to visit, she irritably remarked, "Pier Giorgio could choose a better moment to be ill."[72]

That something was drastically wrong should have been obvious. A few days into his increasingly ominous symptoms, for example, he had dragged himself to his grandmother's room to be present as she died. He used the wall for support and collapsed to the floor three times as he struggled along the corridor. But he was a young, athletic mountain climber—they thought he had nothing more than a passing fever. What he had, however, was a virulent form of polio. Within six days, he was dead.

"Poor Giorgio!" his sister and only sibling said of the family's neglect. "Nothing was spared him."[73] She was referring not so much to his physical suffering, which was intense, as to their indifference to his needs and their clumsy handling of his last hours. When they left him behind to go to the grandmother's funeral, he was already paralyzed from the waist down, "and no one in the house knew it."[74] He never complained when the doctor refused his request for morphine, saying it would be too dangerous, or when his mother refused to let his friends come in to sit with him in his few remaining hours. When it became clear that the end was near, she wouldn't even admit his good friend the archbishop into the room, and Pier Giorgio ended up making his last confession to a priest with whom he had serious disagreements.

His parents and Luciana, his sister, were shattered by his death but, as Luciana said later, they never really knew him. His night watches in prayer, his daily Bible reading, his devotion to Mary, the mother of Jesus—all this escaped their notice, though they knew he went to daily Mass. His secret and extensive life of service to the poor, especially, was entirely hidden from them. They had never bothered "to find out where his interests lay or what was their inspiration. We did not know, even up to the eve of his death," his sister wrote, "that if he was late for a meal it was because he had given away all his money to some poor person, or his jacket to another."[75]

That Pier Giorgio was well-loved among the destitute became evident as news of his death spread and as the poor began to arrive to pay their respects. To the family's astonishment, they descended on the house, streaming through to spend a moment at his bedside where he was laid out for the wake. The funeral drew a huge crowd—the poor, his vast network of friends, the well-to-do colleagues of his parents—who jammed the streets and pressed in around his coffin as his friends carried it on their shoulders to the church. Traffic came to a standstill. "I have never seen and will never again see so many tears at a funeral," a newspaper reporter wrote.[76]

Always Mercy

Pier Giorgio's charism for mercy was apparent even from childhood, making his family's failure to grasp his true nature that much sadder. He was visiting a kindergarten one day—he was about four years old—when he noticed a child covered with eczema sitting alone at lunch, isolated for fear of contagion. Pier Giorgio went over, sat with him, and shared his spoon even though the teacher tried in vain to move him away. On another occasion, he answered the door to find a poor woman begging, accompanied by her barefoot child. He quickly stripped off his shoes and socks and gave them to the child.

By the time Pier Giorgio was eighteen and a university student, he had joined the St. Vincent de Paul Society. In a typical week, he seemed to be everywhere on behalf of the poor. On Monday, an early biographer said, it would be

> a room found for a poor old woman whose landlord had just thrown her out on the street; on Tuesday it is boots for a young man who cannot go to work because he has no footwear; on Friday it is a bed in a hospital, obtained after two days trying, for a consumptive in wretched circumstances. [77]

On Saturday, it was new living quarters for a blind war veteran—and helping him and his family of five children move in. "God alone knows how many visits he made and with what prodigality he spent his money, his time and his heart."[78]

His parents were on the receiving end of Pier Giorgio's gift for mercy too, though they didn't recognize it. The Frassati marriage was tense and without affection, maintained only in order to keep up appearances. Alfredo, a senator and the owner of *La Stampa*, the influential, liberal newspaper, and Adelaide, a well-regarded painter, let their contempt for one another set the tone for the family home. Luciana, his sister, described her and Pier Giorgio's childhood as grim. Their mother was hypercritical and emotionally manipulative; Alfredo buried himself in his work and had an authoritarian streak. The two children lived in fear that their parents would separate, and even when he became an adult, Pier Giorgio determined that he would not leave them to themselves. He would have liked to have gone to America, he said, but by that time Luciana had married, and his departure would have left their parents alone.

In spite of the icy home atmosphere, Pier Giorgio felt genuine affection for his parents. He maintained a close relationship with his mother, subduing his naturally exuberant personality so that he wouldn't ruffle her sensitive nature. His father seemed disappointed in him, in part because he was not academically gifted, but Alfredo once said to a friend that "Pier Giorgio leaves me in awe, as though I were dealing with someone older."[79] He customarily greeted his son, at dinner, with "Ciao, Giorgetto bello!" (Hello, handsome Georgie!). "Ciao, pappo!" Pier Giorgio would reply.[80]

His determination to place his parents' needs before his own met a final challenge the month before he died. He had decided to become a mining engineer, motivated solely by a desire to serve miners because they were poor and neglected, and their work was dangerous. As he prepared for his final exams after four years of engineering studies, his father asked him to join him in the family business—to work at *La Stampa*. Actually, Alfredo didn't have the nerve to make the request himself and had a colleague do it. Pier Giorgio had always detested office work, but he asked, "If I do this, will that make Papa happy?" When the intermediary said yes, then Pier Giorgio accepted.

His mother called him her silent son, but Pier Giorgio had learned that silence helped keep the peace. Outside the home, he was gregarious and fun-loving but thoughtful and always concerned for the well-being not only of the poor but also of his many friends. A natural athlete, he thought nothing of making the fifty-three-mile bicycle ride between the house in Turin and the family's summer house in Pollone. He was particularly adept at mountain climbing, and he and his friends—male and female—frequently took off for the nearby Alps for serious climbs. *Verso l'alto*, he scrawled across a photo of himself on a mountaintop—"To the heights." Other photos show him roped for safety and dangling from a rock face or standing on a peak with a pipe clenched between his teeth.

He was their leader, a friend acknowledged—someone to whom they instinctively turned not only when they needed a party organized or someone to round up the wine for a celebration, but when they were upset or depressed or felt they were losing their way in life. "He possessed in eminent degree what [Blessed John Henry] Newman described as 'The gift of sympathy,'" a biographer wrote.[81] He combined that sensitivity with the ability to step up and take action if needed. This was a time of rising fascist sentiment in Italy—Mussolini was coming to power, aided by his thuggish Brownshirts—and on one occasion, fascists broke into the family home in the middle of the night. Pier Giorgio beat them back single-handedly, shouting "Cowards! Assasins!" as he chased them out the door. On another occasion he landed in jail for defending a religious banner while participating in a procession that came under attack from political opponents.

Pier Giorgio determined that his vocation was as a layman in the world, and he joined the Dominican Third Order—the lay arm of the Dominicans—in 1922. He fell in love sometime later but decided against pursuing the relationship as he searched for God's plan for his life. When that plan included his early death, he was ready. A priest who knew him well said, "He was God's, and it is not possible to describe him better than that. He was not a sentimental believer; he was a reasoning man guided by faith, obeying the will of God even unto death."[82]

Pier Giorgio was beatified by Pope St. John Paul II—who had read of him when he himself was a young student in Kraków—in 1990. He was, the pope said in his homily that day, "a man of the . . . beatitudes."[83]

Questions for Reflection

1. The charism of mercy is often associated primarily with serving the destitute. But Pier Giorgio also lived the charism in the heart of his distressing family life. In what ways can you practice mercy today in your family or among those you with whom you live? How do you think Pier Giorgio discerned that his family was a kind of mission territory where he was called to serve?

2. Exercising mercy on behalf of others comes at a cost. What spiritual practices or insights do you rely on when you are confronted with a call to extend mercy? How do you cultivate those practices and pursue those insights ahead of time so that you are ready when you find yourself in a situation that demands mercy?

3. Pier Giorgio's spirituality was seamlessly integrated into his life, which was, in many ways, an ordinary one. How does having a well-rounded personality and thoughtful involvement in the issues of the day serve as an entry point for evangelization and growth in holiness?

CHAPTER TEN

Naturally Supernatural

Edel Quinn

◆

Charism: Missionary

Born September 14, 1907, in Kanturk, Ireland
Died May 12, 1944, in Nairobi, Kenya

Work for the day. The saints never lost time. Live for the day. Life is made up of days. Why lose a moment on the way during a brief journey? . . . Never waste time.

—Edel Quinn[84]

The author Flannery O'Connor once said that "the pious style is a great stumbling block to Catholics who want to talk to the modern world."[85] O'Connor, a devout Catholic, was talking about a particular style of writing. Edel Quinn, her contemporary and a laywoman with a remarkable missionary charism, would easily have seen the missionary implications of O'Connor's remark: a tone and style that speak to the world in one era might not be suitable for another.

No one would ever have accused Edel of having a pious style at odds with modern life. She had all the usual traits you'd expect to find in a missionary—zeal, a strong relationship with God, and a firm grip on Church teaching—but she had something else: a zest for life and an outstanding sense of humor. "She was great fun," Frank Duff, her friend and the founder of the Legion of Mary, said of her. "She laughed her way through everything." A nun who was disagreeing with her about something said with indignation: "Don't start your laughing at me now, Miss Quinn. Just answer me these questions."[86]

Near the end of her life, when she had been a missionary in Africa for nearly eight years and was dying of tuberculosis, a bishop told her that he would arrange "a funeral worthy of the great apostle that you are."

"One would expect those tender words of the bishop to open the gates of emotion," Frank Duff said. That she would allow herself "the little luxury of giving into tears. . . . But no. . . . She burst into uncontrollable laughter! It was so typical of her."[87]

Well before Pope St. Paul VI wrote his groundbreaking

apostolic exhortation *Evangelii Nuntiandi* [Evangelization in the Modern World], Edel had captured its spirit. She was not one of those "evangelizers who are dejected, discouraged, impatient or anxious." She was one of those "whose lives glow with fervor, who have first received the joy of Christ, and who are willing to risk their lives so that the kingdom may be proclaimed."[88]

And she did risk her life, as a single woman traveling around East and Central Africa on behalf of the gospel—through crushing heat and torrential downpours, in poor health, over rutted paths turned to mud, oblivious to danger from lions and other wildlife that shared the road. Thirty years before Pope St. John Paul II delivered his stirring homily at the inauguration of his pontificate, Edel Quinn had lived out his plea: "Do not be afraid. Open wide the doors for Christ."[89]

Change of Plans

Edel had intended to be a contemplative nun and had been accepted by the Poor Clares in their Belfast monastery when the diagnosis of tuberculosis cut short that plan. Given how her life played out, it is reasonable to wonder if a cloistered vocation would have suited her temperament.

From the start, she was known as highly energetic and a leader, at the center of any group. One of her grade school teachers recalled that Edel would take off from school on her bike, racing down a hill at full speed—and then, still flying,

turn around to wave, signaling, "I've got this." She was athletic—as were her three sisters and one brother—and close to
her devout mother, Louise, who shared the family penchant
for outdoor activity and took a swim in the sea every morning.

She loved her father, Charles, too, though it became apparent that he lacked his wife's strength of character. He was also
the source of Edel's unusual name. Her father took her to be
baptized a few days after her birth—Edel's mother was still
recovering and unable to attend. She told him to be sure to get
the name right: the baby was to be named Ada after her Aunt
Ada, whose nickname was Adele. Her father, thinking the name
was to be Adele, said so to the priest who, compounding the
bungling with his own bungling, said, "Of course, Edelweiss,
Edel for short."

Not only did the two men between them give the baby a
name never intended by her mother, but as a biographer wrote,
"For the rest of her life, Edel was never quite sure whether her
name was Edel or Edelweiss, whether she was called after her
aunt or a small white Alpine flower."[90]

Her father was a bank manager whose position required
that the family move every few years to wherever in Ireland
the bank needed him next. He was laid-back and "enjoyed a
drink and a flutter on the horses"—a combination that nearly
brought the family to ruin when he was caught embezzling the
bank's money in order to pay off his gambling debts.[91] Edel was
sixteen at the time and a student at a high school in England.
Her parents, no longer able to afford the tuition, summoned
her home and sent her to secretarial school so that she could

get a job to help support the family. The bank (and the Quinns) hushed up the reason for the family's diminished circumstances. To protect its reputation, the bank merely demoted him to a lowly position in Dublin and slashed his salary.

Edel took it all in stride and soon became the de facto head of the family, relied on for her wisdom and unflappable nature. She took a job at a tile import business and became friends with the owner, a young Frenchman named Pierre. "She was always smiling," he said of her, "and Edel Quinn's smile was something to remember."[92] They spent time together after work, sometimes playing tennis or dancing—she was an "incredibly" graceful dancer, Pierre said. "To dance as she did . . . she must have loved dancing." She did love dancing as well as all sports, excelling particularly at golf and tennis.

She also excelled at her work, gradually taking on managerial duties at the office. On one occasion, she stood up to dock-workers who took advantage of a situation to demand more money for unloading tiles at the dock. It's likely that they mistook the young, attractive, well-dressed Edel—she had a flair for fashion—as a pushover. At any rate, they threatened to call in a lawyer, but Edel was unyielding, and they backed down.

She could handle dockworkers easily enough, but she was taken by surprise when Pierre proposed marriage. She turned him down—she already had the convent in her sights—prompting Pierre to write, years later, that "I knew her and I didn't know her at all."[93] What he didn't know, aside from her unexpected choice of vocation, was the depth of her spiritual life. Nobody really did.

Forward in Faith

The fellow commuter who dubbed Edel "the Seapoint Sprinter" captured her spirit, if not the reason for her sprint. She attended Mass early every morning before work, and the only way she could catch the train to the office afterward was by running to the Seapoint station.

"The Word made flesh"—the Eucharist—"was for her the centre of all reality on earth," her best friend, Mary Walls said, but Edel pursued holiness using the means

> common to all fervent Catholics, . . . very frequent confession, daily meditation, spiritual reading, visits to the Blessed Sacrament, the Rosary and . . . the Little Office of the Blessed Virgin Mary, the constant practice of interior recollections, of self-denial, fraternal charity, and all the other Christian virtues.[94]

Not that anyone ever heard her talk about her spiritual practices or make any reference at all, at any time, to her interior life. Even Mary Walls, who went on to become a Carthusian nun, said that "she never told me anything about her own spiritual life."[95] Edel "maintained an impenetrable reserve regarding her interior," Frank Duff wrote.[96]

"She believed in keeping the 'Secret of the King,'" as Mary put it, but Mary thought she knew why. She was "convinced, judging from [Edel's] conversation and her life, that she received special graces in prayer. . . . Like Our Lady, she kept all the interior graces she received, 'pondering them in her heart.'"[97]

Edel had a deep devotion to the mother of Jesus, and when she encountered the Legion of Mary a few years after Pierre's proposal, the organization proved to be a natural fit. Although she didn't yet know it and was still on track for the convent, the course for her life was now set: it would be the Legion.

Founded in Dublin in 1921, the Legion of Mary was a laity-led Marian association that was in some ways a counterpart to the St. Vincent de Paul Society. While the St. Vincent de Paul Society offered material as well as spiritual aid to the needy, the Legion of Mary was devoted solely to spiritual works of mercy. Organized around weekly group meetings in local units known as praesidia, the Legion sent Catholics out in pairs into the homes of the lonely, elderly, ill, poor—anyone and everyone interested in learning about the faith or in need of prayer and friendly conversation.

Edel agreed to lead the praesidium devoted to befriending the prostitutes crowding Dublin's slums. She helped out at Sancta Maria Hostel, the halfway house the Legion established for women trying to leave the streets, and quickly became a favorite of the women there. Her gift for sympathetic listening and faith-based encouragement won many—almost all the women were Catholics who had somehow managed to hang onto their faith in spite of their brutal circumstances. Her gift for fun helped ease the atmosphere—she provided endless entertainment in the form of skits, charades, music (she played the piano), and dancing lessons.

A hemorrhage followed by the fateful diagnosis of tuberculosis brought her plans for the convent to an end. She spent nearly a year in a sanatorium, watching as other patients recovered and left, while she never gained ground. Finally, convinced that the enforced inactivity was doing her no good, she checked out of the facility and returned home. She didn't have a clear sense of direction, but her Legion of Mary work had helped to hone her missionary charism. She had been exposed to a wide variety of people and their needs, and been given the tools—the Legion's structure and collaborative approach—to address them.

On to Africa

Once back in Dublin, she resumed her work with the Legion, but her colleagues wouldn't allow her to do anything demanding. She complained, saying she felt they had her "sitting up in a coffin."[98] Her chance to break out and do the hard stuff came from an unexpected quarter: Africa. The Legion had no presence in East or Central Africa, but when an invitation came in from a bishop there, Edel was ready. The climate would work against her delicate health, but the leaders of the Legion agreed to let her go, knowing that her genius lay in a "sense of mission which seemed to be necessary to her."[99]

She would be starting from scratch, but as Frank said when sending her off, "she would start a prairie fire there." And she did. Over nearly eight years, she established and nurtured hundreds of praesidia from Uganda to the island of Mauritius, far off the coast of Africa in the Indian Ocean. Her willingness to go to Mauritius was remarkable in itself—she said she was the world's worst sailor; but more to the point, the thousand-mile journey took place during World War II, when every other boat in the Indian Ocean was being torpedoed.

She worked closely with missionaries in both remote and urban locations, keeping in mind one particular goal: to help establish the Church in Africa so that Africans themselves could assume responsibility for the evangelization of their continent. This idea was so essential "that if it be not brought into full play, the Church cannot be universally extended or solidly founded," Frank wrote.[100] The Legion did this by strengthening the faith life of its individual members and helping their members take the faith to others. This laity-led evangelization was before its time, especially in Africa where only priests and nuns were expected to do "Church work."

Edel did the work against all odds. She was most at home with Africans and was often unimpressed by white settlers who tended to treat Africans, Indians, and Asians with disdain. Almost everywhere, she encountered obstacles to forming praesidia of mixed races, although occasionally she managed to do so. Some missionary priests and nuns were hostile to her efforts, some felt the Legion was not "African" enough, some were worn-out and indifferent—but many embraced the Legion "as the only effective way of making apostles out of ordinary men and women."[101]

Her final collapse came after a mission trip undertaken when she could barely walk and was overcome by fatigue. Returning to Nairobi, she rested in the garden of the convent where she lived when she was not on the road. She didn't seem to realize that she was dying. She asked a nun who was with her, "What's wrong with me, Mother? I feel very sick." A priest arrived in time to anoint her, and shortly after, she said, "Jesus" several times and gently slipped away.

Testimonies soon poured in, especially from missionaries who recognized that through her work she really did help to make apostles out of ordinary men and women. Bishop John Heffernan of Zanzibar, who had known her from the start of her service in Africa, said the following of her:

> After a year of Miss Quinn's work, the atmosphere of my diocese had changed. Without any noise, she had brought a germ of life. . . . The renewal of Catholic vitality was noticeable in the Legionaries who were gradually transformed. Priests, too, experienced . . . a spiritual metamorphosis. One could almost feel the passing of grace. What she brought to us was Catholic action in all its purity. . . . She did everything without constraint, joyfully, naturally, and with irresistible humor. She was naturally supernatural.[102]

As Frank Duff remarked, she "ranks with the great builders of the Church in Africa."[103]

Her cause for canonization is underway.

Questions for Reflection

1. Edel seemed to discover her missionary charism gradually, through her life experiences. Do you sense God speaking to you through your experiences? How? Are you willing to change course if he seems to be closing one door and opening another?

2. Edel's cheerfulness and sense of humor helped her to radiate the joy of the gospel. What role do joy and a sense of humor play in your life? In what ways might humor be a measure of humility? How can humor help to lower barriers when sharing the gospel?

3. Not everyone has a missionary charism, but every Catholic has a responsibility to share the gospel with others. Have you had opportunities to do so? Do you pray for opportunities to share the faith and for the courage to speak up?

Afterword
saints continue to transform our world

I really enjoyed reading Sherry's book. It made me think about the person I owe my vocation to the priesthood to. Even though he wasn't a layperson, Fr. Remigius McCoy, a Missionary of Africa (White Fathers), was a lowercase "saint" who also happened to be my maternal grandfather's cousin. From the late 1920s until 1992, Fr. McCoy evangelized the Dagaaba and Sissala Tribes in Ghana.

My first memory of Fr. McCoy dates back to 1964, when he accompanied the first bishop of the Diocese of Wa, Ghana, Bishop Peter Poreku Dery, for a mission appeal at our parish in Detroit. He was among the first cohort of catechumens to be baptized by Fr. McCoy in the early 1930s.

Fr. McCoy would continue to visit our family in Detroit over the years as he made mission appeals to support the many projects he developed to help his beloved Dagaaba and Sissala people. The projects ranged from building a chapel in one of the neighboring villages, schools, and eventually a hospital that outshone any other in the region. Our family looked forward to his visits which, though usually unannounced, were always welcome.

It was with great anticipation that I traveled to visit him in his compound in Jirapa in 1985. I wanted to hear more of the stories in the place where they happened. There, he told me about his mission work.

He came to Jirapa in 1929. He and his two confreres built several small round mud huts, including a clinic and a temporary chapel. The missionaries first made friends with the "paramount chief" of the village and then began to tell the story of Jesus to the villagers, who were also somewhat astonished at the healings that occurred through the work of the clinic. Over the next few years, they made a reasonable number of catechumens in Jirapa and throughout the region.

Then came the great drought in 1932. The dry season did not end at the usual town, and the poor farmers began to get anxious. The witch doctors and rainmakers offered gifts and sacrifices to the spirits, all to no avail. As the drought continued, anxiety turned into terror.

The catechumens of a neighboring village importuned the chief and elders to go to the mission to see if the missionaries could make it rain. The troop of the elders brought with them many gifts, but Fr. McCoy told them to take them away, saying that he was not a magic worker who could make it rain. "But," he said, "God can give you rain, if you ask him." The chief told him that they had no hope except in him. "Alright," he said, I will pray for rain, but you must also pray with me." He explained to them that God was different than the juju magic they depended on, and then he led them sentence by sentence in a simple prayer for rain. After about half an hour or so in the chapel, the elders returned to their village. When they reached the borders of their village, rain fell in torrents. But only on their village.

Word began to travel throughout the wider region. Delegations came from as far as fifty miles away to pray with the priest at this chapel. He said that every village that sent elders to Jirapa to pray received rain either on the day or the day after. By the end of the harvest, there were about ten thousand Dagaaba and Sissala people camped outside the compound who simply asked, "Who is this God that loves us so much that He would send us rain for free?"

Fr. McCoy was dubbed by his confreres of the Missionaries of Africa as the "rainmaker." His parishioners called him the "father of the rains."

He died in August of 1993, and though he died in Canada, I came to know that his funeral in Jirapa lasted for more than three weeks. Today the Diocese of Wa, Ghana, comprises 350,000 Catholics who owe their faith to the simple yet bold proclamation of the gospel of Jesus Christ brought to them by Fr. McCoy.

May God bless all those who read this book, and may the wonderful stories inspire all of us to be open to our charisms and God's voice in our lives.

—**Most Reverend Michael J. Byrnes**, S.T.D., Archbishop of Agaña, Guam

Notes

1. Liliana Usvat, "Antony Gaudi and Mathematics," *Mathematics Magazine*, http://www.mathematicsmagazine.com/Articles/AntonyGaudiandMathematics.php.

2. Austen Ivereigh, "Gaudi, the Blessed," *GodSpy*, https://oldarchive.godspy.com/culture/Architect-Gaudi-the-Blessed-by-Austen-Ivereigh.cfm.

3. Stanley Meisler, "Gaudi's Gift," *Smithsonian Magazine*, July 2002, https://www.smithsonianmag.com/arts-culture/gaudis-gift-65213577/.

4. Juan Manuel González-Cremona, *Towards the Beatification of Antoni Gaudí*, http://gaudibeatificatio.com/files/docs/GAUDI-BOOK.pdf, 20.

5. "Biography of Antoni Gaudí," *Casa Batlló*, https://www.casabatllo.es/en/antoni-gaudi/.

6. Ivereigh, "Gaudi, the Blessed."

7. "The Symbolism of Light in Gaudi's Work," *Casa Batlló*, https://www.casabatllo.es/en/news/the-symbolism-of-light-in-the-work-of-gaudi/.

8. Ivereigh, "Gaudi, the Blessed."

9. Pope Benedict XVI, Homily, Dedication of the Sagrada Família, November 7, 2010, http://w2.vatican.va/content/benedict-xvi/en/homilies/2010/documents/hf_ben-xvi_hom_20101107_barcelona.html.

10. Meisler, "Gaudi's Gift."

11. Pope John Paul II, Letter to Artists, April 4, 1999, 16, https://
w2.vatican.va/content/john-paul-ii/en/letters/1999/documents/
hf_jp-ii_let_23041999_artists.html.

12. Lancelot C. Sheppard, *Barbe Acarie, Wife and Mystic: A
Biography* (New York, NY: David McKay Co., 1953), 193.

13. Sheppard, 32.

14. For a deeper look at the Catholic revival that marked this
period in French history, see my book *Becoming a Parish of
Intentional Disciples*, (Huntington, IN: Our Sunday Visitor,
2015), chapter 1, "The Generation of Saints," 11-28.

15. Robert P. Maloney, CM, "The Beautiful Acarie," *Vincentiana*,
vol. 41, no. 3 (May 1997), https://via.library.depaul
.edu/cgi/viewcontent.cgi?referer=https://www.google
.com/&httpsredir=1&article=1989&context=vincentiana.

16. Barbara B. Diefendorf, *From Penitence to Charity: Pious
Women and the Catholic Reformation in Paris* (New York,
NY: Oxford University Press, 2002), 105.

17. "Saint of the Day," April 30, *St. Patrick Catholic Church*,
http://www.saintpatrickdc.org/ss/0430.shtml.

18. Maloney, "The Beautiful Acarie."

19. "What Brought a Japanese Aristocrat to Christ?" *Aleteia*,
December 28, 2017, https://aleteia.org/2017/12/28/what
-brought-a-japanese-aristocrat-to-christ/.

20. Boniface Hanley, OFM, *Eight Women Who Made a
Difference: With Minds of Their Own* (Notre Dame, IN: Ave
Maria, 1991), 209.

21. Hanley, 210.

22. Paul Glynn, SM, *Smile of a Ragpicker: The Life of Satoko Kitahara* (San Francisco, CA: Ignatius Press, 2014), 63.

23. Glynn, 63.

24. Glynn, loc. 1097, Kindle.

25. Thomas E. Auge, *Frederic Ozanam and His World* (Milwaukee, WI: Bruce Publishing Company, 1966) 42.

26. Javier Chento, "20th Anniversary of the Beatification of Frederic Ozanam, a Lay Saint for Our Times," *Vincentian Family Office*, August 22, 2017, https://famvin.org/en/2017/08/22/20th-anniversary-beatification-frederic-ozanam-lay-saint-times/.

27. Auge, 4.

28. Shaun McCarty, SJ, "Frédéric Ozanam, A Layman for Now. Chapter 2," *Vincentians*, September 10, 2016, http://vincentians.com/en/frederic-ozanam-a-layman-for-now-chapter-2/.

29. Boniface Hanley, OFM, *Ten Christians: By Their Deeds You Shall Know Them* (Notre Dame, IN: Ave Maria Press: , 1979), 88.

30. Auge, 46.

31. Hanley, 80-81.

32. Hanley, 82.

33. Auge, 143, 146.

34. George Cowley, "Georges Vanier," *Online Encyclopedia of Canadian Christian Leaders,* https://www.canadianchristianleaders.org/leader/pauline-vanier-2/.

35. Mary Frances Coady, *Georges and Pauline Vanier: Mercy Within Mercy* (Collegeville , MN: Liturgical Press, 2016), 5.

36. George Cowley, "Georges Vanier," *Convivium*, November, 4, 2016, https://www.convivium.ca/voices/71_georges_vanier.

37. "Letter Written by Georges P. Vanier after His Visit to the Buchenwald Concentration Camp," *Vanier College*, https://www.vaniercollege.qc.ca/about/history/georges-vanier-letter.html.

38. Jean Vanier, *In Weakness, Strength: The Spiritual Sources of Georges P. Vanier, Nineteenth Governor-General of Canada* (Toronto, Canada: Griffin House, 1975), 29.

39. Coady, 83.

40. Jean Vanier, *In Weakness, Strength*, 17.

41. Deborah Cowley, "Pauline Vanier," *Convivium*, November 11, 2016, https://www.convivium.ca/voices/73_pauline_vanier.

42. Coady, 48-49.

43. Coady, 70.

44. Jean Vanier, *An Ark for the Poor*, (Toronto, Canada: Novalis, 1995), 35.

45. Coady, 107.

46. Coady, 98-99.

47. Jean Vanier, *An Ark for the Poor*, 20.

48. Coady, 82.

49. Jean Vanier, *An Ark for the Poor*, 37.

50. W. J. Howlett, "A Fortuitous Find of Some Letters of Ira B. Dutton, the Brother of Joseph of the Lepers of Molokai," American Historical Society, https://www.jstor.org/stable/44209102?seq=1#page_scan_tab_contents.

51. Pat McNamara, "A Servant of the Lepers: Brother Joseph of Molokai," *Patheos*, October 8, 2012, https://www.patheos.com/catholic/servant-lepers-pat-mcnamara-10-09-12.

52. Vital Jourdan, SS CC, *The Heart of Father Damien*, (Milwaukee, MN: Bruce Publishing 1955), 344.

53. Gavan Daws, *Holy Man: Father Damien of Molokai* (New York, NY: Harper and Row, 1984), 167.

54. "Ira Barnes 'Brother Joseph' Dutton, *Find a Grave,* https://www.findagrave.com/memorial/28457601/ira-barnes-dutton.

55. Jourdan, 346.

56. "Dutton, Ira Barnes," *Vermont in the Civil War,* http://vermontcivilwar.org/get.php?input=50008.

57. Pat McNamara, "A Servant of the Lepers."

58. "Brother Joseph Dutton: Servant of God," *Saint Damien of Molokai Catholic Church & Parishes,* http://damienchurchmolokai.org/wp/brother-joseph-dutton/.

59. Madeleine Delbrêl, *We, the Ordinary People of the Streets* (Grand Rapids, MI: Eerdmans, 2000), quoted by Jacques Loew, Introduction, 34.

60. Colleen Dulle, "Who Is Madeleine Delbrêl—the 'French Dorothy Day' Pope Francis made venerable this weekend?" *America Magazine*, February 1, 2018.

61. Madeleine Delbrêl, *We, the Ordinary People of the Streets*, https://www.communio-icr.com/files/43.4_Delbrel_We_the _Ordinary.pdf, 697.

62. Madeleine Delbrel, *We, the Ordinary People of the Streets*, 29.

63. Gosia Brykczyńska, *Colours of Fire: The Life of Hanna Chrzanowska* (Hershey, PA: William R. Parks, 1914), 101.

64. Brykczyńska, 19.

65. Brykczyńska, 20, 21.

66. Brykczyńska, 5.

67. Brykczyńska, 27.

68. Brykczyńska, 74.

69. Brykczyńska, 102.

70. Brykczyńska, 103.

71. Robert Claude, SJ, *The Soul of Pier Giorgio Frassati*, trans. Una Morissy, BA (Cork, Ireland: Mercier Press, 1958), 40.

72. Luciana Frassati, *A Man of the Beatitudes: Pier Giorgio Frassati* (San Francisco, CA: Ignatius Press, 2001), 156, 157.

73. Frassati, 158.

74. Frassati, 156.

75. Claude, 118.

76. Christina Siccardi, *Pier Giorgio Frassati: A Hero for Our Times*, trans. Michael J. Miller (San Francisco, CA: Ignatius, 2016), 318.

77. Claude, 33.

78. Claude, 33.

79. Claude, 94.

80. Siccardi, 68.

81. Claude, 14.

82. Siccardi, 134.

83. Pope John Paul II, Homily, Beatification of Pier Giorgio Frassati, May 20, 1990, *L'Osservatore Romano*, May 28, 1990, 9.

84. "Words of Life from Edel Quinn," *Arlington Legion of Mary,* http://www.arlingtonregia.com/legionsaints/edelwol.html.

85. Flannery O'Connor, *The Habit of Being* (New York, NY: Farrar, Straus, Giroux, 1988), 135.

86. Frank Duff, "Edel Quinn," *E-Catholic 2000,* https://www .ecatholic2000.com/cts/untitled-140.shtml.

87. Duff, "Edel Quinn."

88. Pope Paul VI, *Evangelii Nuntiandi* [Evangelization in the Modern World], December 8, 1975, 5, http://w2.vatican.va/ content/paul-vi/en/apost_exhortations/documents/hf_p -vi_exh_19751208_evangelii-nuntiandi.html.

89. Pope John Paull II, Homily, Inauguration of His Pontificate, October 22, 1978, w2.vatican.va/content/john-paul-ii/en/ homilies/1978/documents/hf_jp-ii_hom_19781022 _inizio-pontificato.html.

90. Desmond Forristal, *Edel Quinn 1907–1944* (Dublin, Ireland: Dominican Publications, 1994), 2.

91. Forristal, 5.

92. Leon-Joseph Suenens, *Edel Quinn: Envoy of the Legion of Mary to Africa* (Dublin, Ireland: C. J. Fallon Ltd., 1952), 21.

93. Forristal, 19

94. Sr. Mary Celestine Walls, "I Knew Edel Quinn," *Faithful Catholics,* https://sites.google.com/site/faithfulcatholics/Home/devotion-to-mary/legion-of-mary/edel-quinn/i-knew-edel-quinn.

95. Walls, "I Knew Edel Quinn."

96. Duff, "Edel Quinn."

97. Walls, "I Knew Edel Quinn."

98. Duff, "Edel Quinn."

99. Duff, "Edel Quinn."

100. Duff, "Edel Quinn."

101. Forristal, 99.

102. Suenens, 240-241.

103. Suenens, 256.

About the Catherine of Siena Institute

When I'm teaching about charisms, I often reassure people that God won't suddenly remove a long-term charism and replace it with something totally different. No one goes to bed a happily married administrator and wakes up in the morning as a celibate exorcist (though that might be the basis for an odd situation comedy). But in the last two decades, I've been reminded that God can throw you some astonishing curveballs. God will not radically alter your charisms while you sleep, but he's quite capable of altering your *life* with dizzying speed.

Over a Memorial Day weekend of out-of-the-blue rapid-fire developments in 1997, Fr. Michael Sweeney, OP, of the Western Dominican Province, and I decided to cofound the Catherine of Siena Institute. Our mission from the beginning was "equipping parishes for the evangelization and formation of lay Catholics." From its beginnings as a small ministry of the Western Dominican Province, the Institute has grown into a global organization working directly with over 170,000 people in 1,000 parishes and 200 dioceses on 5 continents.

I had been writing and rewriting the Called & Gifted discernment process for three years beforehand, so the Called &

Gifted workshop was our first major offering. In the 22 years since, over 100,000 Catholics and non-Catholics have attended Called & Gifted workshops all over the world. For many, it has been a life-changing event as they heard, often for the first time, that they are called by God and that in Baptism and Confirmation, they have been given charisms that empower them to answer the call. God's call is not merely for our own sake but for the sake of others and the world. As one woman put it, "I used to think I wasn't worthy to kiss the sandals of Jesus, and now you are telling me I am to put them on and walk as if they fit—that I stand in his place with my daughter and my friends and my coworkers. *This . . . is revolutionary.*"

God sent another curveball in 2012 with the viral response to my book, *Forming Intentional Disciples: The Path to Knowing and Following Jesus (FID).* Not only did *FID* become a Catholic bestseller, but it opened new doors to work with thousands of Catholic pastors, leaders, and parishioners who desire to see their parishes and dioceses become places where disciples are made, formed, and sent into the world as missionary disciples.

FID, its companion *Becoming a Parish of Intentional Disciples,* and *Fruitful Discipleship* sparked the demand for more Catherine of Siena Institute formation tools that could help parishes fulfill their evangelizing mission. Here are a few examples:

- *Making Disciples*, a multi-day experience for disciple makers at parish and diocesan levels, was first offered in 2004 in Colorado Springs. It has since grown into a three-seminar series: MD 101, 201, and 301. *Making Dis-*

ciples is continually updated as we learn more about the realities of evangelizing in a time of tremendous change and the growing need for parishes to be responsive and innovative in mission.

- To expand the global reach of Called & Gifted, a streaming video option was introduced in the fall of 2019 along with expanded training for local teams to support both the workshop, gifts interviews, and discernment small groups.

- *Ananias Training* debuted in 2018 in response to the need to help parishes equip evangelizers with a practical knowledge of the discipleship thresholds, how to hold threshold conversations and how to tell one's own story as well as proclaim Jesus' story. It includes a video-based day retreat on *The Great Story of Jesus* that can be used as an evangelizing tool in a wide variety of settings and groups.

- We run the *Forming Intentional Disciples* Facebook forum, a closed, international, 10,000+ member, 24/7 support and discussion group for Catholics interested in evangelization and making disciples in the twenty-first century. To join us, search Facebook for *Forming Intentional Disciples Forum*, and then click on the icon that says, "I want to join." Answer the questions that pop up, and we'll admit you.

- I have begun speaking and writing on my next major project that will focus on the theology, practice, power, and impact of Jesus' Real Presence in the Eucharist, Adoration, and intercessory prayer in the twenty-first century. We are realizing afresh how crucial these are in reaching Catholics and non-Catholics who are not yet intentional disciples or do not know where to begin with an evangelization strategy.

For more information about all that we offer and our global event calendar, check out the Catherine of Siena Institute website at **www.siena.org**.